D0952264

PRAISE FOR
A FIELD GUIDE TO
A HAPPY LIFE

"Pigliucci reimagines Epictetus's *Handbook* (a.k.a. the *Enchiridion*) and updates it for the twenty-first century. The result is a work more timely than ever, for it warns us of the dangers of superstition while it reminds us that reason and virtue are essential to happiness. Pigliucci speaks directly to us as readers and justifies his updates along the way. He thereby invites us to treat Epictetus and this very book as a reasonable guide rather than as an oracle from on high."

—Brian E. Johnson, Fordham University

"This is a bold, contemporary updating of Stoicism for the present day. Taking the ancient Stoic Epictetus as his inspiration, Pigliucci has rewritten Epictetus's *Handbook* in order to update it, make it more relevant to a modern audience, but also to ensure that the core Stoic ideas shine through. The result is what Pigliucci calls Stoicism 2.0. This is a manual for living for those who approach the ancient Stoics as guides, not masters."

—John Sellars, author of *Stoicism*

"An engaging introduction to the Stoic life through an updated version of Epictetus's *Handbook*. An unusual and helpful feature is an appendix in which Pigliucci highlights his modifications of the original Stoic text to take account of modern thinking."

—Christopher Gill, author of *Greek Thought*

A FIELD GUIDE TO A HAPPY LIFE

•

53

BRIEF LESSONS FOR LIVING

MASSIMO PIGLIUCCI

BASIC BOOKS

New York

Copyright © 2020 by Massimo Pigliucci

Cover design by Chin-Yee Lai
Cover image © Verisstudio / Shutterstock.com
Cover copyright © 2020 Hachette Book Group, Inc.

Hachette Book Group supports the right to free expression and the
value of copyright. The purpose of copyright is to encourage writers
and artists to produce the creative works that enrich our culture.

The scanning, uploading, and distribution of this book without permission
is a theft of the author's intellectual property. If you would like permission to
use material from the book (other than for review purposes), please contact
permissions@hbgusa.com. Thank you for your support of the author's rights.

Basic Books
Hachette Book Group
1290 Avenue of the Americas, New York, NY 10104
www.basicbooks.com

Printed in the United States of America

First Edition: November 2020

Published by Basic Books, an imprint of Perseus Books, LLC, a
subsidiary of Hachette Book Group, Inc. The Basic Books name
and logo is a trademark of the Hachette Book Group.

The Hachette Speakers Bureau provides a wide range of authors for speaking
events. To find out more, go to www
.hachettespeakersbureau.com or call (866) 376-6591.

The publisher is not responsible for websites (or their
content) that are not owned by the publisher.

Print book interior design by Amy Quinn.

Library of Congress Cataloging-in-Publication Data
Names: Pigliucci, Massimo, 1964– author.
Title: A field guide to a happy life : 53 brief lessons for living / Massimo Pigliucci.
Description: New York : Basic Books, 2020. | Includes bibliographical references.
Identifiers: LCCN 2020009777 | ISBN 9781541646933
(hardcover) | ISBN 9781541646940 (ebook)
Subjects: LCSH: Conduct of life. | Epictetus. Manual. | Stoics.
Classification: LCC BJ1531 .P55 2020 | DDC 171/.2—dc23
LC record available at https://lccn.loc.gov/2020009777

ISBNs: 978-1-5416-4693-3 (hardcover); 978-1-5416-4694-0 (e-book)

LSC-C

10 9 8 7 6 5 4 3 2 1

*To my wife, Jennifer, whose love and support
are making it easy to live a happy life.*

CONTENTS

PART I

BETTING ON THE PHILOSOPHER-SLAVE

EPICTETUS AND ME

My life changed instantly, and for the better, in the fall of 2014.[1] At least, an important, impactful, and positive change began then, and is continuing now. The trigger was my first reading of a philosopher I had never heard of, despite the fact that he was a household name for eighteen centuries or thereabout: Epictetus. The words in questions were,

> I have to die. If it is now, well then I die now; if later, then now I will take my lunch, since the hour for lunch has arrived—and dying I will tend to later.[2]

It blew my mind. Who the heck was this first-century guy who in two sentences displayed both a delightful sense of humor and a no-nonsense attitude toward life, and death? We don't really know much about him. Not even his real name. "Epíktetos" (ἐπίκτητος) in Greek simply means "acquired," since he was a slave, born around the year 55 in Hierapolis (modern-day Pamukkale, in western Turkey). He was bought by Epaphroditos, a wealthy freedman and secretary to the emperor Nero.

Sometime after moving to Rome, Epictetus began to study Stoic philosophy with the most prestigious teacher of the time, Musonius Rufus. That may have helped him on the occasion of a defining episode in his life, when he became crippled. Origen tells us how Epictetus handled it:

> Might you not, then, take Epictetus, who, when his master was twisting his leg, said, smiling and unmoved, "You will break my leg;" and when it was broken, he added, "Did I not tell you that you would break it?"[3]

Eventually Epictetus obtained his freedom and began to teach philosophy in Rome. At first, it didn't go too well. Referring to an episode that happened to him while he was expounding philosophy in the streets of the imperial capital, he recounted to one of his students,

> You run the risk of [someone] saying, "What business is that of yours, sir? What are you to me?" Pester him further,

and he is liable to punch you in the nose. I myself was once keen for this sort of discourse, until I met with just such a reception.[4]

Apparently, he wasn't annoying just to people in the street. Like many other Stoics before and after him, he had a dangerous tendency to speak truth to power, so the emperor Domitian exiled him in the year 93. Undaunted, he moved to Nicopolis, in northwestern Greece, and established a school there. It became the most renowned place to learn philosophy in the entire Mediterranean, and a later emperor, Hadrian, stopped by to visit and pay his regards to the famous teacher.

Epictetus, just like his role model, Socrates, did not write anything down, focusing instead on teaching and talking to his many students. Thankfully, one of them was Arrian of Nicomedia, who later became a public servant, military commander, historian, and philosopher in his own right. The only two sets of teachings we have from Epictetus are Arrian's notes, collected in four books of *Discourses* (half of which are unfortunately lost) and a short handbook, or manual, known as the *Enchiridion*.

Epictetus lived a simple life, unmarried and owning few things. In his old age he adopted a friend's child, who would have otherwise been "exposed" to death, and raised him with the help of a woman. He died around 135 CE, approximately eighty years old—a remarkable age for the time, or any time, really.[5]

Back to my own discovery of Epictetus. I was positively stunned. Why had I never come across his writings before? Or even his name (such as it is)? I was fairly well acquainted with the other major Stoics, particularly Seneca and Marcus Aurelius, but Epictetus didn't come up even during my graduate studies in philosophy! His star may have been eclipsed among modern professional philosophers, occupied as they too often are in precisely the sort of logical hairsplitting that the sage from Hierapolis disdained.[6] But his influence has been constant throughout the centuries, and continues to grow.

Not only did the writings and teachings of Epictetus, and in particular his handbook, influence the last of the Roman Stoics, the emperor Marcus Aurelius, but the *Enchiridion* was translated and updated by Christians throughout the Middle Ages, and used as a manual of spiritual exercises by monks in monasteries. The first printed edition, translated in Latin, was the work of Angelo Poliziano in 1479, who dedicated it to the Medici of Florence. The book arguably reached its popular height in the period 1550 to 1750, between the Renaissance and the Enlightenment. The first English translation (based on a French original) was by James Sandford in 1567. The Jesuit missionary Matteo Ricci translated it in Chinese in the early seventeenth century. John Harvard bequeathed a copy to his newly founded college in 1638, and Adam Smith, Benjamin Franklin, and Thomas Jefferson all had copies in their personal libraries.

But Epictetus's manual appears in unexpected places throughout history. Shakespeare has Hamlet declaim, "There is nothing either good or bad, but thinking makes it so" (Act 2, Scene 2), which is a slight paraphrase of *Enchiridion* 5. Epictetus is also mentioned in François Rabelais's *Pantagruel*; in *The Life and Opinions of Tristram Shandy, Gentleman* by Laurence Sterne; in *A Portrait of the Artist as a Young Man* by James Joyce; and he is paraphrased by John Milton.

More recently, David Mamet and William H. Macy, who introduced the acting method known as practical aesthetics, list Epictetus among their sources. And so does Albert Ellis, the founder of rational emotive behavior therapy, the forerunner of cognitive behavioral therapy, the most successful evidence-based modern type of psychotherapy.

The 1998 novel *A Man in Full*, by Tom Wolfe, features a character whose life (in prison) is turned around by reading the *Enchiridion*. James (Bond) Stockdale, a fighter pilot who served and was captured in Vietnam, received the Medal of Honor, and later ran as vice president of the United States in 1992, tells us in his memoir that Epictetus saved his life during his years of imprisonment, torture, and solitary confinement in the infamous "Hanoi Hilton."

And have you heard of the Serenity Prayer? It was written in the early part of the twentieth century by the American theologian Reinhold Niebuhr, and is commonly adopted by twelve-step organizations like Alcoholics Anonymous. It goes like this:

> God, grant me the serenity to accept the things I cannot change,
>> Courage to change the things I can,
>> And wisdom to know the difference.

The same idea is also found in Solomon ibn Gabirol, an eleventh-century Jewish philosopher, as well as in Shantideva, an eighth-century Buddhist scholar. The earliest known version of it is from the very beginning of the *Enchiridion*, as we shall see shortly.

Arrian, the student of Epictetus to whom we owe both the *Enchiridion* and the *Discourses*, wrote to his friend Lucius Gellius,

> When [Epictetus] was speaking, he plainly had no other aim than to move the minds of those who were listening toward what is best. . . . When Epictetus himself was speaking, the listener was compelled to feel just what Epictetus wanted him to feel.[7]

The world is a better place because Arrian preserved Epictetus's teachings. Countless have benefited from his insights into how the cosmos work and how to behave toward others. More broadly, the endurance of Stoicism across the millennia is a testimony to the basic pragmatism of its doctrines and to the usefulness of adopting Stoic philosophy as our compass to live a eudaemonic life, a life worth living.

I'm sure Arrian sought to preserve Epictetus's words in part out of respect, love even, for his master. Nineteen centuries later, it is the same respect and (indirect) love that move me to propose this Field Guide, an attempt to update the *Enchiridion* and, with it, the entire Stoic system. My hope being that countless more people may benefit from the power of this philosophy to change lives for the better.

Some people will reasonably disagree with my proposed updates, just as the ancient Stoics disagreed among themselves about what was and was not entailed by their philosophy. Naturally, even this current version will eventually be made obsolete and in need of further changes by the continuous expansion of human understanding. Which is what the Stoics themselves predicted and welcomed.

One thing that hasn't changed much, though, is human nature itself, which is why words written for and by people who lived two millennia ago still resonate so clearly with us today. Those people did not have smartphones and social media, airplanes and atomic weapons. But they loved, hoped, feared, lived, and died pretty much like we do today. And so long as those basic facts about humanity stay true, Stoicism will remain one of our most powerful tools for enduring life's inevitable setbacks and for enjoying more deeply life's many gifts—if we use humility and wisdom as our guides.

HOW TO USE THIS BOOK

This *Field Guide to a Happy Life* is a *vademecum*; that is, it falls into a long tradition of portable books that people would want to "carry with them" (the literal translation of the Latin: *vade* = go; *mecum* = with me). I chose the title "Field Guide" because life happens "in the field," so to speak, not in the peace and quiet of libraries or one's own living room.

The first section of the book, which you are reading now, is meant as a general introduction to Stoicism and to Epictetus in particular. Use it whenever you need a quick refresher of the basic ideas.

The most crucial section is the central one, the actual Field Guide, which you can read with no background at all about Stoicism, Epictetus, or even philosophy. It comprises fifty-three units, each paralleling a similar unit of the original manual. In a number of cases, the substance of my version is not different from that of Epictetus's version, in which case what you get is simply Epictetus rendered in modern language, and using more relatable examples.

But there are also twenty-seven units, that is, just about 50 percent of the total, in which my thinking diverges more or less sharply from that of Epictetus. Those are the crucial bits where I gradually carry out my project of updating Stoicism for the twenty-first century and beyond, what I ambitiously call Stoicism 2.0. The topics treated in the diverging units are still those with which Epictetus was concerned, but the way I approach them is different.

How different? I will discuss that in the third and last section of the Guide. Think of that section as a handy summary of how modern Stoicism—at least in my version—diverges from the "original," while of course keeping in mind that Stoicism has constantly been altered and updated, through the centuries and the millennia.

I.3

STOICISM 101

The story of Stoicism begins near the closing of the fourth century BCE, when a Phoenician merchant by the name of Zeno of Citium loses everything in a shipwreck and arrives at Athens. Diogenes Laertius tells us what happened next:[1]

[Zeno] was shipwrecked on a voyage from Phoenicia to Piraeus with a cargo of purple. He went up into Athens and sat down in a bookseller's shop, being then a man of thirty. As he went on reading the second book of Xenophon's Memorabilia, he was so pleased that he inquired where men like Socrates were to be found. Crates passed by in the nick of time, so the bookseller pointed to him and said, "Follow yonder man." From that day he became Crates's pupil.

Xenophon's *Memorabilia* is a book about the life of Socrates, and Crates of Thebes was a prominent Cynic philosopher. That word, "Cynic," did not mean what it means today (neither did "Stoic," for that matter), but rather indicated a philosophy dedicated to a minimalist lifestyle and the cultivation of virtue, or the excellence of one's moral character. Zeno studied with Crates and a number of other philosophers, eventually deciding, around 300 BCE, to begin teaching on his own. He purposely chose to teach in an open space lined by columns, just off the main Athenian marketplace, the Agora. The space was known as the Stoa Poikile, or painted porch. Hence the term still used today: "Stoicism."

Zeno's new philosophy taught that we should live "according to nature," meaning not that we should run naked into the forest to hug trees (though there is nothing wrong about that), but rather that we should take human nature seriously. According to the Stoics, the most important characteristics that distinguish the human species from every other organism on earth are that we are capable of reason (which doesn't mean that we are always, or even often, reasonable) and that we are highly social. From these observations they derived the fundamental axiom of their philosophy: a good human life, what the ancients called a eudaemonic life, is one that is lived by applying reason to the betterment of society.

Consequently, the Stoics were cosmopolitan, thinking of the entirety of the human race as one big brotherhood and sisterhood. Unlike most other philosophical schools of their time, the Stoics believed that women's intellectual capacities were equal to those of men. They developed a very practical philosophy of life, an approach that is sometimes referred to as "the art of living."

One way to begin to think, and act, like a Stoic is by using the so-called cardinal virtues as a moral compass for everything you do. There are four cardinal virtues: practical wisdom, courage, justice, and temperance. They are defined in the following way:

Practical wisdom is the knowledge of what is truly good for us, as well as what is truly bad for us. For the Stoics, this boils down to the understanding that the only thing that is good is virtue, or excellence of character, and the only thing that is bad is vice, or defect of character. Everything else—including the sort of things most people desire, such as health, wealth, fame, and so forth—is "indifferent," meaning that they may be reasonably "selected," or preferred, but are morally neutral. In other words, being wealthy may be nice, but it does not make you a good person; being poor may be uncomfortable, but it doesn't make you a bad person; or vice versa.

Courage is the propensity to act morally in the face of danger, or in situations where one would rather stay put and not expose oneself to criticism or retaliation.

Justice means acting in a way that is fair toward other people, treating them as you would want to be treated by them, and always respecting their dignity as human beings.

Temperance is the inclination to do things in right measure, neither too little nor too much.

One crucial aspect of Stoic doctrine is that the four virtues are highly interdependent, because they are all aspects of a more fundamental virtue, which can simply be referred to as wisdom (in the broad sense). One cannot, for instance, be courageous and yet unjust. If you brave a dangerous or uncomfortable situation for the wrong reason, you are not being morally courageous, you are just engaging in braggadocio, or worse.

For example, let's say that you witness your boss at work harassing a coworker. Should you intervene? The Stoic approach is to deploy the four virtues simultaneously. Practical wisdom reminds you that to intervene in this sort of situation is good for your character, while nonintervention is bad for your character, so that's a yes vote. Courage demands that you step in despite the fact that your boss may retaliate against you. Justice says that you would not want to be harassed, and that you would appreciate someone else's taking your defense. So logic demands that you do the same for others. Finally, temperance suggests the proper way to respond to your boss: neither by quietly whispering your objection under your breath (too little), nor by charging at him and punching him in the face (too much).

While the Stoics devised a number of specific practical exercises[2] to become better human beings—from journaling to meditating to engaging in mild forms of temporary self-deprivation—a constant, mindful application of the four virtues gets you a long way toward improving your character and being helpful to what the Stoics call the human cosmopolis.

EPICTETEAN PHILOSOPHY 101

pictetus lived several centuries after Zeno, and he introduced a number of innovations in Stoicism, including a radically new way of practicing it. This should not be surprising, as philosophies (and, indeed, even religions) are dynamic sets of ideas that are constantly challenged internally and externally. Consequently, all philosophies change and adapt themselves for practical use and relevance in their own time.

In fact, just two generations after Zeno, Chrysippus of Soli, one of the greatest logicians of the ancient world, had made so many adjustments to the original Stoicism that Diogenes Laertius comments, "But for Chrysippus, there had been no Porch," meaning that he significantly transformed and improved the Stoic system.[1] Both before and after that the Stoics were challenged by the Epicureans and by the Academic Skeptics, and saw the evolution of three major periods of their philosophy (rather unimaginatively referred to as the early, middle, and late Stoa).

One of the innovations that Epictetus brought to Stoicism is the development of a sophisticated "role ethics," an approach to ethics based on taking seriously the different roles we all play in life: the general role of a human being in society at large; roles that we choose for ourselves, such as being a father, or a friend; and roles that the circumstances assign to us, such as being a son or daughter. Epictetus's role ethics was in turn an elaboration and advancement on a similar concept developed by Panaetius, a philosopher of the middle Stoa, who lived from 185 to 109 BCE.

There are two crucial aspects of Epictetean philosophy that I wish to focus on here, because they are pivotal to understanding, and properly using, this Field Guide: the so-called dichotomy of control and the three disciplines of Stoic practice.[2]

The dichotomy of control is introduced by Epictetus right at the beginning of the *Enchiridion*:

Some things are within our power, while others are not. Within our power are opinion, motivation, desire, aversion, and, in a word, whatever is of our own doing; not within our power are our body, our property, reputation, office, and, in a word, whatever is not of our own doing.

In modern language, this boils down to the notion that we are in charge only and exclusively of our deliberate judgments, our endorsed opinions and values, and our decisions to act or not to act. Nothing else. We do not even control much of our mental life, which is largely automatic, according to modern cognitive science. Everything else—especially externals like health, wealth, reputation, and so forth, we can try to influence, but ultimately depend on a combination of other people's actions, as well as on the circumstances. Just like the abovementioned Serenity Prayer says, then, the fundamental insight here is that we need to cultivate the wisdom to be able to distinguish between what is and what is not under our control, the courage to tackle the first, and the equanimity to accept the second.

The dichotomy of control was not Epictetus's original invention, although he made it into the centerpiece of his brand of Stoicism. Compared to his predecessors, Epictetus articulated the dichotomy of control most clearly, dedicated time to exploring its consequences, and consistently applied it to his teachings. But one can find earlier versions of the notion in Seneca, whenever he contrasts virtue (which is up to us) with externals (which are up to Fortune).[3] The dichotomy of control is also implied in Cicero's *On the Ends of Good and*

Evil. While Cicero—who lived between 106 and 43 BCE—was an Academic Skeptic, not a Stoic, he was sympathetic to Stoicism and learned about it firsthand from the middle Stoic Posidonius. Indeed, Cicero proposed what I think is still the best metaphor I've come across to properly understand the dichotomy of control:

> If someone were to make it their purpose to take a true aim with a spear or arrow at some mark, their ultimate end, corresponding to the ultimate good as [the Stoics] pronounce it, would be to do all they could to aim straight: the person in this illustration would have to do everything to aim straight, yet, although they did everything to attain their purpose, their "ultimate end," so to speak, would be what corresponded to what we call the Chief Good in the conduct of life, whereas the actual hitting of the mark would be in our phrase "to be chosen" but not "to be desired."[4]

Consider carefully what is and is not under the archer's control. She is in complete charge of selecting and taking care of the bow and the arrows; of practicing shooting at a target; of selecting the precise moment in which to let the arrow go. After that, however, nothing is under her control: the target, an enemy soldier, say, may become aware of the arrow and move out of range; or a sudden gust of wind may ruin the most perfect shot.

It comes naturally to think that the dichotomy is too strict: surely there are a number of things that fall in between the two "control" and "no control" categories. This led modern Stoic William Irvine to propose a "trichotomy" comprising control, influence, and no control.[5] To my mind, this suggestion is a mistake, one that could end up destroying one of the foundations of Stoicism. Think of it this way. As clearly illustrated in Cicero's passage, everything we influence can in turn be broken down into the two components of control and no-control: practicing archery belongs to the first, a gust of wind to the second; the choice of when to let the arrow go to the first, a sudden evasive maneuver by the target to the second. And so on. Indeed, when we say that we can "influence" an outcome what we mean is precisely that *some components* of the action are up to us and some are not—by breaking our understanding of things into parts, we see that just what Epictetus stated is true.

The most important passage in Cicero's metaphor is the very last one: hitting the mark is to be chosen, but not to be desired. Obviously, the archer intends to hit the target, that's the whole point. Similarly, we prefer to be healthy rather than sick, wealthy rather than poor, and so forth. But because these outcomes are not entirely under our control—and assuming we have done our best regarding what is under our control—then our self-worth should not depend on hitting the target (or being healthy, wealthy, etc.). In life, sometimes we win and sometimes we lose, so equanimity toward outcomes (we "choose" them but we don't "desire" them) is the only reasonable attitude to cultivate.

The second crucial aspect of Epictetus's philosophy with which we will concern ourselves here comprises his so-called **three disciplines**, which essentially substitute for the four virtues discussed above as our moral compass in life. The three disciplines are as follows:

THE DISCIPLINE OF DESIRE (AND AVERSION)

According to the Stoics, we have a tendency to desire (and have aversion to) the wrong things, and this is a major cause of our unhappiness.[6] Specifically, we desire the by now familiar set of externals, including health, wealth, reputation, and so on. That is, we desire things that are, ultimately, not under our control. Similarly, we are averse to losing those same things. The problem is, Seneca reminds us, that by desiring what is not under our control, we put our happiness in the whimsical hands of Fortune.

That is not a smart gamble. Far better it is to redirect our desires toward the things that we actually control, in other words, our considerate judgments. Why? Because that way our chances of living a eudaemonic life are left entirely to our own efforts, not to the vagaries of Fortune. We can still sensibly prefer to be healthy, wealthy, and so forth, but we accept the basic reality that—regardless of our efforts—sometimes we get those things and sometimes we don't. And even when we do get them, such possession is transitory, because everything changes all the time.[7]

How on earth do we begin to realign our desires and aversions so drastically? By way of the two basic steps of Stoic practice, which have also been the inspiration for modern cognitive behavioral therapy: a deliberate, reasoned decision (the cognitive step), and the implementation of changes in our life aimed at habituating ourselves to the new pattern (the behavioral step). For instance, every time you face a challenging task or situation, make a habit to reflect on it and write down a list of aspects of the task or situation that are under your control, as well as a list of those that are not under your control. Then, use the lists to guide your attention, time, and efforts on elements of the first list: aspects of the task or situation that are under your control. Remind yourself, by way of a short mantra, if need be, that elements you've assigned to the second list are not up to you. Just like with anything else, from driving a car to playing an instrument, to going to the gym, mindful efforts do the trick over time: the more you do it, the easier it gets.

THE DISCIPLINE OF ACTION

A fundamental aspect of human nature, according to the Stoics, is that we are eminently social beings. We can survive, under extreme circumstances, on our own, but we don't thrive other than in relation to others. Indeed, a major source of well-being for humans is found in meaningful relationships we have with fellow members of the cosmopolis—the worldwide community of all human beings—particularly with friends and family. The discipline of action, then, is concerned with learning how to properly act in the world, both toward ourselves and toward others.

Here is where the abovementioned role ethics of Epictetus becomes relevant, as we go through life learning how to balance the various roles we play in society. A typical pertinent Stoic exercise is the evening philosophical diary, a way to develop the habit to reflect on where we have gone wrong, what we have done well, and what we could improve.

Epictetus explicitly advises us in this respect: "Admit not sleep into your tender eyelids till you have reckoned up each deed of the day—How have I erred, what done or left undone? So start, and so review your acts, and then for vile deeds chide yourself, for good be glad."[8] The goal is to implement the same two steps, cognitive and behavioral, with the aim of becoming better human beings, which means becoming more thoughtful and more helpful to society at large, the human cosmopolis.

THE DISCIPLINE OF ASSENT

There is an important way in which the discipline of desire and action connect: they both require good judgment on our part. Accordingly, the third discipline, of assent, is meant to improve our faculty of judgment, what Epictetus refers to as *prohairesis*. In a sense, in fact, the major goal of Epictetus's version of Stoic training is to improve our capacity to arrive at good judgments. The reason for this goes back to the early Stoa. Both Cleanthes (the second head of the Stoic school) and Chrysippus (the third) had put forth the notion that wisdom *is* the ability to properly assess our impressions. "Impression" is a technical Stoic term meaning our first take on either our sensorial perceptions or our internal thoughts and feelings.

For instance, if I'm strolling down the old streets of Rome and I see some gelato in a shop window, my first impression will likely be that the gelato is good and that I *need* some of it. Right now. However, my *prohairesis* immediately kicks in and says to the impression, "Hold on a minute here, maybe you are not what you pretend to be, let's consider things for a moment, before we act." Indeed, upon reflection, I find a number of good reasons not to walk into the shop to get the gelato: it isn't going to be good for my waistline, and therefore my health; and moreover, I am on my way to dinner with my wife, and I certainly don't want to spoil my appetite. As a result of this more careful consideration of the impression, I decide to forgo the gelato. (I must immediately admit, however, that sometimes the initial impression trumps my *prohairesis*. As it turns out, I'm not a sage yet!)

The situation I just described is precisely how we practice refining our judgment: We take the course of action that is the opposite of the message in the famous commercial. We don't "just do it," we pause, think about it, and we'll likely see that we don't actually need to "do it." Again, implement these steps over and over and you'll get better at your judgment calls. Which in turn will make it easier for you to realign your desires, as well as to properly interact with other people. The three disciplines, while they are presented sequentially for pedagogic purposes, in reality always act in concert: in life you simultaneously have to deal with your desires and aversions, to act in the world, and to arrive at the best judgments you can.

Not at all coincidentally, the central part of this book, which you are about to read, is largely organized along the three disciplines of Epictetus. Section 1 of the Field Guide introduces the dichotomy of control; sections 2–29 deal with the discipline of desire and aversion; sections 30–41 with the discipline of action; sections 42–45 with the discipline of assent; sections 46–52 concern more generally how to live philosophically; and section 53 presents a short selection of my favorite quotes from Epictetus.

PART II

THE FIELD GUIDE

II.1

SETTING THINGS STRAIGHT

WHERE YOU LEARN THE MOST IMPORTANT
AND PRACTICAL LESSON OF THEM ALL

1

SOME THINGS ARE ENTIRELY UP to you, while other things are not entirely up to you. It's surprising to realize what falls into each category. Entirely up to you are your considered judgments, your opinions, your goals, your adopted values, and your decisions to act or not to act—in essence, what you decide upon after reflection and deliberation. Not entirely up to you is pretty much everything else, but especially your body, your relationships, your career, your reputation, and your wealth—in essence, things you can influence but the outcome of which also depends on others.

How is this possible? Is it not the case that other people can influence your opinions and judgments, and so on, while you can influence the state of your body, relationships, and so forth? Yes, it is. But in the end, for the first category the buck stops with you; for the second the buck stops elsewhere. Others may affect—or even try to manipulate—your opinions, or change your values. Nevertheless, your opinions and your values belong to you. Conversely, you may take care of your body, and yet an accident or disease may cripple you; you may love others and they may not love you back; you may do everything right at your job and still get fired; you may be a good person and yet your reputation may suffer from malicious rumors; you may handle your money with care, and still the market may crash and wipe out your wealth.

Remember, then, that the only things truly yours are those that are entirely up to you. Everything else is on loan from the universe, and the universe may recall such loans at a moment's notice, in any number of ways. It follows that if you put a lot of stake into things that are not ultimately up to you, you are bound to suffer, to envy, to be disappointed, and in general to depend on the vagaries of Fortune. Yet, if you focus your efforts on what is up to you, you will go through life with serenity, approaching all that comes with equanimity, never envying anyone, and never being disappointed by the turning of the cosmos.

With time and practice, you will be able to strike a wise balance between the effort you put into what is truly up to you and what is not. It is human to prefer loving relationships, a good job, a bit of money, and all the rest, so in the beginning of your training, it will be difficult to achieve such balance. But don't give up just because you slip up here and there. Progress is the result of sustained effort. Just as Rome wasn't built in a day, the development of your better self requires years of practice, likely, the rest of the years you have left. Yet, that very progress is the only sure guarantee of freedom and happiness.

Here is an important piece of advice: Every time you have a strong desire for something (or a strong aversion to something, which amounts to the same thing, really), train yourself to talk to the source of that desire (or aversion) and to say, "You are just an impression, and may not be at all what you portray yourself to be! Let me take a closer look and see what's what." Then put the impression to the crucial test and ask yourself, is it ultimately up to you, or not? If yes, focus all your resources on it. If not, you may prefer it, but you should not attach your sense of worth to it. It is reasonable that you prefer to be healthy, wealthy, loved, etc. But your worth as a human being does not depend on such things. If you get them, fine; if you don't, also fine. Do not sell your soul cheaply, my friend.

TRAINING YOUR DESIRES AND AVERSIONS

WHERE YOU BEGIN TO REORIENT YOUR
LIKELY MISGUIDED DESIRES AND AVERSIONS

2

AN INSIGHT INTO THE HUMAN condition: you control far less than you think, and you likely have mistaken ideas about what you do, in fact, control. This widespread ignorance is at the root of much unhappiness: you desperately desire things that—ultimately—are not up to you, while at the same time you neglect to put effort into the things that, as a matter of fact, are up to you. The right strategy, therefore, is to recalibrate your priorities along the following lines.

First and foremost, your attention should be trained on your judgments, your decisions, and your efforts, that is, the things that are truly up to you. Second, your attitude toward externals—that is, everything else—should be that of an archer: although hitting the target is the goal, you should keep in mind that once the arrow leaves your bow, its course may be altered due to a sudden gust of wind, or an unforeseen movement by the target itself.

So what can you do? Shift your goals from the external to the internal: repeat to yourself that your objective is not to hit the target, but to deliver the best shot of which you are capable; it is not to get the job promotion, but to be the most deserving candidate for it; it is not for someone else to love you, but to be the most loving person you can be. If you redirect your attention and desires in this fashion, you will be happy and serene.

EVERYTHING YOU THINK YOU OWN is not actually yours: not your favorite mug, not your house, not your job, not even your partner or child. At some point you will lose them, in one fashion or another. You should prepare yourself for this, and in the meantime be keenly aware that you have them and thankful for it. It is easy to do this with material possessions: if your favorite mug breaks, tell yourself, "It was a mug, I knew it could break." You should then gradually work your way to more difficult things: if you lose a great deal of money because the market has a downturn, tell yourself, "It was invested money, I knew it could be lost."

When it comes to human beings, do not be callous, and yet apply the same principle and cultivate equanimity in all your doings: if a friend moves away, you should tell yourself, "I have known all along that people move, he is still my friend." And this also for the most difficult thing of all: if a loved one dies before you do, tell yourself, "I have known all along that one of us had to go first, I am thankful of every moment I spent with them."

FOR EVERYTHING YOU SET OUT to do, keep in mind what is most likely to happen, and rehearse ahead of time how you will react.

Let's say you are going to a show, and someone near you begins to make some fuss. There is no sense in getting upset, because you knew from the beginning that people often act this way at shows. Instead, upon leaving your home you should tell yourself, "I want to enjoy the show, but I also want to keep my inner peace and my harmony with others." If you are lucky, you will get to do all of that, but how are you going to keep peace and harmony if the simple fact that someone makes a fuss has the power to shatter you to pieces?

So when faced with the annoying neighbor, by all means try your best to persuade him to behave pro-socially, but ultimately maintain awareness of what you can control: "My goal was to enjoy the entertainment but also to keep inner peace and harmony with humanity. This time I may not achieve the first, but at least I have the other two." Apply this practice to everything you set out to do, and you will be on the path to a serene life.

5

YOU ARE NOT DISTURBED BY things in themselves, but by your judgments of things. Look around you and notice that people react differently to the very same occurrences, which means that they judge them differently. For some, losing a job is a catastrophe. For others, it is an opportunity to seek a new path forward. Most people shy away from pain, but some voluntarily expose themselves to it in pursuit of a higher goal, such as completing a marathon or passing a difficult exam.

The same goes even for death itself: it cannot be a bad thing, because you will not be there when it arrives. And yet, fear of death keeps human beings slaves of whoever or whatever they believe may help them avoid the inevitable, be that a religious or a technological cult.

Now here are three stages of wisdom: the unwise person blames other people for what are, in the end, her own judgments about things; the person who is making progress does not blame others, but only herself; the wise person does not blame even herself.

DO NOT CONGRATULATE YOURSELF FOR things that don't really belong to you. Do you have a nice car? The merit goes to the engineers who conceived it. Do you have a nice house? The merit goes to the architects who designed it. If you say "look what a beautiful car I have," you are taking credit for an incidental, and certainly not for something that makes you a better human being.

What is actually yours, then? The proper use, through your considerate judgment, of what life loans to you. You have a nice car. Fine. What are you going to do with it that is helpful to the human cosmopolis? You have a nice house. Great. Are you going to open it up to friends and neighbors, are you going to make it the nest of a thriving family? Those and only those are the sorts of things that make you a good human being, and of which you should be proud.

7

HAVE YOU EVER BEEN ON a cruise? If so, you will know that when you are allowed ashore you may entertain yourself by looking around and doing some shopping, but you should always be aware of when the ship will depart, lest you end up stranded where you don't belong.

The same goes with life. It's fine to enjoy its pleasures and to entertain yourself a little. But you should always keep in mind that at some point the voyage will be over, since it does not last forever. When the time comes, be ready, and make sure that you look back and do not find that you have misspent your shore leave.

The best way to avoid this is to ask yourself from time to time what is important, and to act accordingly. Thus, some people only begin to truly live when they are already old. Others, do not begin at all.

Do not demand that things happen in the way you want them to happen. That is childish. The universe does not owe you anything, and does its business without concern for you.

Instead, remember that what is truly up to you is to do your best in order to achieve your goals, while also keeping in mind that actually achieving those goals is not entirely up to you. In life sometimes you will win, sometimes you will lose, and at other times you will get off with a tie.

Cultivate, then, an attitude of equanimity toward externals. Be glad and appreciate when they work in your favor; don't get mad when they don't.

9

If you are sick, your body will be hampered, but not so your will. You can manage to be a decent human being even when sick. Lack of money will hamper your ability to do certain things, but not your will. You can manage to be a decent human being even if you are poor.

The same goes for every other condition imposed by externals: those things that may constrain your actions one way or another will not constrain your will. That is the only sense in which you are free, and in which your freedom is up to you.

HERE IS A GOOD WAY to navigate your life: remember that for anything that happens to you, you will find the resources within you to deal with it.

Say, for instance, that you are tempted by lust; you will discover your ability for temperance. Or maybe you are experiencing pain; you will find that you have a capacity for endurance. Or perhaps someone has insulted you; you will use your reserve of patience to deal with the fool.

Practice your abilities regularly and you will not be overwhelmed by the happenings of life.

11

YOU SHOULD GO THROUGH LIFE as a traveler who stops at an inn: never regarding anything as truly yours, but as on loan from the universe.

Has someone taken away your property? That was not yours in the first place (because nothing is), so you gave it back to the cosmos. "But it was taken from me by a bad person!" It makes no difference to you. You have given it back, it is someone else's problem now, and they will face whatever consequences, beginning with a stain on their conscience.

This also holds for the more difficult things: A loved one has died? They were never yours, but on loan from the universe, and the universe has taken them back. How this happened is of little consequence. When it happened was not up to you either. Be grateful, instead, that they were around for a while, and that they have made your life better because of their presence.

IF YOU WISH TO MAKE progress, set aside thoughts like these: "If I don't spend more time on my investments, I will not make as much money." Or: "If I don't push myself forward at work, I will not be promoted." Or: "If I don't try to impress people, I will not be well regarded." For it is better to have less money, to miss out on a promotion, or not to be well regarded, than to lose your serenity and your self-worth.

Practice this by beginning with little things: some wine is spilled on you. Do not get upset. Instead, say to yourself, "This is the small price I pay in order to keep my inner peace and harmony with others." Gradually, move on by practicing bigger things: some of your money has been stolen. It is not worth getting upset, because you would simply add a self-inflicted injury to whatever has already happened.

13

IF YOU WISH TO MAKE progress, be happy to be considered clumsy or foolish by others with regard to externals. Don't try to impress them with your knowledge, since you truly have little of it. If they think you are someone of importance, don't trust their judgment. You know better. Socrates was the wisest man in Greece on the grounds that he realized that he knew nothing.

The thing is, it is difficult to make progress on refining your judgment when your attention is consumed by the pursuit of externals. Indeed, the very fact that you still think that pursuing externals is important is a measure of your scarce progress. You can't devote much energy to becoming wealthy and wise at the same time; or famous and wise; or successful and wise. It is one or the other. And you ought to know which one.

As DIFFICULT AS IT MAY be, you need to accept that your children, your companion, your friends, and indeed yourself are not going to live forever. This is not a sad fact, it is a fact. The sadness is entirely a construct of your mind. You are foolish if you wish these things not to be the way they are, because it is not in your power to change them.

Similarly, if you wish your colleagues not to be occasionally annoying, or politicians not to be corrupt, or wealthy people not to be greedy, you are a fool, because that is their nature. In general, if you wish people to be different from what they are, you are a fool.

By contrast, if you do not want your desires to be thwarted, then train yourself to desire only things that are up to you, that is, your own judgments, opinions, and values. And nothing else.

If you do desire something that is not up to you, then you make yourself a slave to other people or to circumstances. If you want money, then you'll be the slave of people who can grant you that; if you want fame, then you'll be the slave of people who can bestow that upon you (and just as easily take it away); and so on for any external whatsoever.

Your freedom is in your hands: desire only what is up to you and be averse only to things you can change for the better.

15

HERE IS AN ANALOGY FOR how to conduct your life: Imagine you are at a dinner party. A dish is being passed your way? Great! Take from it with moderation, because others are awaiting their turn. Does the dish by mistake bypass you? Don't greedily reach for it, and do not be upset. It will come around again. And at any rate, you won't starve if you do not sample from it. Has the dish not come yet? It's okay, you can wait and enjoy conversation with your neighbors in the meantime.

This very same attitude you can apply to your family, relations, friends, career, wealth, and so forth. Touch everything lightly, enjoy it while it is within your reach, and do not regret it when it is gone, since that is the nature of things.

PEOPLE ARE DISTRAUGHT BY LOSSES and what they truly believe are misfortunes. Some money has been lost in a bad deal. Someone has lost their job. Or one of their children goes abroad. Or their partner dies. What I just described are facts. The degree to which they are also horrible, or unbearable, is up to each individual's judgment. Some judge one way, others another way.

You will remind yourself of this and train yourself to react to your own adversities with equanimity, keeping in mind that the universe works neither for you nor against you. It just goes on regardless of you.

However, when you interact with others, do not belittle their distress or grief. And indeed, console them as it seems appropriate and efficacious to them. But do not make the mistake of thinking that their judgment about externals is necessary, or appropriate.

17

HAVE YOU EVER PLAYED POKER? Life is like that. You don't get to decide which hand to play, that's up to Fortune, who is blind. You may get a straight flush, or just one pair. Or something in the middle, like three of a kind. No matter, what counts is how you play the hand you have been dealt. If you are not a good player, you can lose even with an excellent hand. And if you are good, you can do quite a bit with what other people may consider a bad hand.

So in life. It is not up to you if you are born rich or poor, smart or somewhat dense, handsome or ugly. But it is very much up to you to make the best of it. That is the measure of your excellence as a human being.

DON'T BE SUPERSTITIOUS. YOU CANNOT read your future in signs from the stars, cards, tea leaves, or psychics.

Besides, no matter what the universe has in store for you, it is up to you to make the best of it, whether it concerns your health, your property, your reputation, or your relations. Let it, therefore, happen as it may; you are ready.

19

THE SURE WAY TO WIN contests is to enter only those in which you are guaranteed to win. The only contest that qualifies is that for becoming a better person. Nothing else.

So when you see someone who is famous, or powerful, or well regarded in any other way, don't be confused by it, and do not think that the person is necessarily happy. If it is true that the only good things are those that are up to us, then there is no room at all for envy or emulation.

You should not desire to be famous, rich, or powerful, but to be free. And the only way to be free is not to attach your well-being and self-esteem to things that are not up to you, such as fame, wealth, and power.

SOMEONE HAS INSULTED YOU? YOU mean, rather, that you allowed them to insult you.

Because regardless of their intention, what they say is just air moving between the two of you. Their words become an insult only if you regard them as such. Otherwise, they are the uttering of a fool.

Try, therefore, not to be bewildered by appearances, and instead take a break from the situation, put some distance between yourself and the immediate impression. That way you will find that it is easier to retain command of your ruling faculty, your ability to reason.

21

MEDITATE FREQUENTLY ON ADVERSITY, AND especially on death, which will reach everyone, including you.

If you do this, you will be far less likely to entertain degrading thoughts, or attach overeager desires to anything at all.

IF YOU TRULY WISH TO embrace the philosophical life, be ready for others to make merciless fun of you. They will say that your head is in the clouds, or that you think yourself superior to them.

On your part, make sure that your head is *not* in the clouds, and most certainly do not feel superior to anyone. If you behave according to your philosophy, people will eventually see it, appreciate it, and possibly even admire it, though this is not the reason why you pursue this way of life.

And lastly, if you merely talk and do not act accordingly, you will be made fun of twice over, and deservedly so, too!

23

DO NOT MAKE THE PURSUIT of externals your chief goal. As soon as you do that, you have left philosophy, and all your efforts are ruined.

Certainly it is preferable to be educated than not, or to have a bit of money than not, and so forth. But these are incidentals, they can easily distract you from your goal.

So be happy to be a practitioner of philosophy in everything, and if you'd like to appear so to others, make sure you appear to be so to yourself in the first place. That will be enough.

THIS IS THE SORT OF thing that should cause you no distress at all: "I will be discredited and live as a nobody." The reason for this is that being discredited is a matter of other people's opinions, and those are not up to you. What is up to you is this: did you do anything discreditable? Similarly, it is no business of yours to worry about whether you will become powerful or influential, or even whether you will be admitted at a place of entertainment. Those things are not up to you, after all. Incidentally, what do you mean that you will be a nobody? You shall be somebody in the proper domain of action, that is, when it comes to your own judgments and decisions.

"But I will not be able to assist my friends and family." What do you mean by that? Your friends may not be able to receive money from you, or other material assistance. But who told you that those things were up to you in the first place? And if you do not have those things, most surely you cannot give them to others, so no fault lies with you.

"But I can make an effort to get money and other things, so that I can assist my friends and family." Of course you can, provided that you do so in a manner that is consistent with the preservation of your integrity and self-respect. If you can get those things that way, by all means do it. But if you have to lose sight of what is truly good for you in order to acquire such things, you would be most unreasonable, and even foolish, to choose that path. Moreover, what would you rather have, some money or a good friend? Work then on becoming the latter; the former may or may not come as the universe allows.

"But my country depends on me, and it will go unassisted." To begin with, your true country is the whole of the human cosmopolis, and that's where your first allegiance should lie. Second, again, what sort of assistance do you have in mind? Your country will not have buildings and works of art that you provided? Neither will it receive health care from a teacher, or education from a doctor. What is enough is that everyone perform their duties, whatever they may be, and within whatever constraints may apply. If you were just to provide your country, or society at large, with another virtuous citizen, that would be enough. It follows that you are not useless, or rather that it is up to you not to be useless.

"What place, then, shall I hold in society?" Whatever place is compatible with the preservation of your integrity and virtue. But if, in your eagerness to do something for society, you lose either of these, how can you be truly useful?

So, YOU DID NOT GET invited to a certain dinner party, or to be a member of a certain circle of people. If these are good things, then be happy that someone else got it and wish them luck. If they are not good things, then why are you complaining? The fact is, you cannot compete for externals such as these without engaging in the proper means to obtain them. Whoever got invited to that dinner or that circle did what was required to get in: flattering those in charge, praising them without believing that praise was due. It follows that it is most unreasonable and even unjust of you to complain about it: you did not want to pay the price, and yet you wished to be admitted?

Consider this: Someone purchases some expensive food and pays the required money. You, however, do not wish to pay the money. You have, therefore, no ground to complain about the fact that you did not get the food. No injustice has been done to you. They have the food, but you get to keep your money.

Similarly, you have not been invited because you did not wish to pay the price of admission: flattering and praising those who you do not think deserve it. If you want to be invited, then pay the required price, if you think it is to your advantage. But if you are not willing to pay, do not go around all sour, complaining that some kind of injustice has been done to you. That would be both unreasonable and foolish. Is it not the case that you have something of yours, in lieu of the invitation? You do: your integrity.

YOU SHOULD REFLECT ON HOW you react to other people's problems and use your own behavior in those circumstances as a guide to how to deal with similar problems when they concern you. For instance, someone's favorite mug breaks, and they become really upset. Naturally, you say, "Do not get distressed, it was just a mug, and it is in the nature of mugs to break." When your favorite mug also breaks, remember those words and repeat them to yourself.

Now apply the same principle to more difficult things. Someone's loved one has died. You console them, in part, by saying, "These things happen, it is natural for human beings to die. Life will continue." This is true, but then when your loved one dies, don't think that the most terrible catastrophe in the universe just happened to you. Life will continue.

The point, understand, is not to be callous about death or catastrophe—yours or anyone else's. The point is to accept what happens with equanimity, because it is natural that it happens, and because it is in your power to decide how to react. Grief is understandable. Desperation is counterproductive.

27

NOTHING IN THE WORLD IS evil or, for that matter, good. The world just is. It is up to us to decide what to do with whatever comes our way.

SUPPOSE SOMEONE TAKES YOUR BODY and gives it to someone else to do as they please. Surely you would be upset, no? So why is it that you don't get upset when other people manipulate your mind so that they can do with it whatever they please?

29

BEFORE YOU EMBARK ON SOMETHING, carefully consider what it entails and what is necessary in order to get it done properly. If you don't do this, then you are bound to start a lot of things and finish nothing.

"I want to compete in the Olympics as a runner." Good for you. But do you have clear in mind what this means? You have to respect the rules, subject yourself to punishing exercise and a hard diet, rigorously follow the counsel of your trainer, abstain from certain pleasures, and so on. Then when the moment comes, you may injure yourself, you may fall on the course, or you may simply lose the race. Are you okay with all of this? If so, then by all means go ahead and begin your training. But if you are not, then don't behave like a child, who today plays at being a doctor and tomorrow at being a fireman, without really doing any medicine or firefighting. Don't allow yourself to get infatuated with ideas if you are not ready to take them seriously, or—worse—because you think people will admire you for it.

Similarly, you want to practice philosophy. But have you considered what this entails, or is it just that you like the idea of being like Socrates? Think carefully about what it is you are about to do, and measure your own nature and inclinations against it, before you embark on it. Do you think you can go after externals the way you do now, and still practice philosophy? That you can crave money, fame, and the rest? That you can get angry? No, you must work on your desires and aversions, train yourself to not get angry with other people, even distance yourself from some of your friends and acquaintances, who may not be good for your training. You may be laughed at, and you need to be prepared to shrug it off. You may not "succeed" at what other people consider important: your career, your wealth, or your reputation. There is no way to get everything in life: You either cultivate your own reason and give precedence to virtue above all else, or you desperately go after externals. You will either give priority to things within you, or to those outside of you. There is a trade-off, and you have to decide which way to go.

Once you have carefully considered all of the above, then and only then should you begin your philosophical path. You will give up much, but you will acquire freedom and serenity. You will be a philosopher, not one of the crowd.

II.3

TRAINING TO ACT IN THE WORLD

WHERE YOU PREPARE YOURSELF TO BEHAVE
JUSTLY TOWARD OTHER PEOPLE

30

YOU ARE A SOCIAL ANIMAL, and whether you like it or not, living in a society comes with certain duties. How do you figure out what these duties are? Just look at the various roles you play. If you are a father, then you have duties toward your children. Conversely, you have duties toward your own parents and toward your siblings. You also have duties, of a different kind, toward your friends, and your coworkers, and the people who work for you, as well as those you work for. Finally, bear in mind always the duty that is most important of all, that of being a good member of the human cosmopolis.

"But," you say, "my mother has been bad to me." Perhaps, but she is your mother nevertheless, and you should concern yourself with how you behave toward her, not how she behaves toward you. "But my brother has done me some harm." What do you mean, "harm"? Has he forced you to change your considered opinions or the values you endorse? No, he can't do that. Then there is no real harm. He may have behaved unjustly toward you, but that is his business. Your business is to behave toward him by considering who he is: your brother.

SOME PEOPLE BELIEVE THAT THE gods have ordained the universe to work in the best possible way, and that those gods care for the lives of human beings. But you are skeptical; you suspect that there really are no gods, and that the universe is the result of natural processes, just like you are. So whatever happens to you is neither just nor unjust, it simply is. This will allow you to look at what happens with proper understanding, knowing that all that happens is the result of a cosmic web of cause and effect of which you are a small but nevertheless integral part. It makes no sense, therefore, for you to blame gods or anything else. It makes much more sense to focus on the things you control and take the rest as it comes.

This can be achieved only if you truly assimilate the concept that you should focus your best efforts on what is up to you: your considered judgments, deliberate opinions, and endorsed values, and nothing else. If you do not do this, then you will keep failing to achieve what is in your power, and continue being distressed by what is not in your power.

It is natural for every living creature to be afraid of and avoid what is harmful, as well as to enjoy and seek what is beneficial. You are a living creature, so you act in the same way. But unlike most other living creatures, you have the power of reason, which allows you to reflect on what is truly good or harmful to you, and enables you to distinguish what is from what appears to be, or from how other people say things are.

Accordingly, other people get upset if, say, they do not get what they think is their fair share of an inheritance. Because they operate under the incorrect assumption that money is a good, while it is only a preferred indifferent. When Romulus and Remus came to blows, and one lost his life as a result, it was because they were under the mistaken impression that power over others is a good thing. Similar mistakes are made by farmers when their crop is not what they expected, or the investor when the market does not behave as he likes, or everyone when they lose a loved one. As if the weather, the markets, or life itself were actually up to them.

Be careful, however: if you understand and internalize the way things are, as distinct from how you would like them to be, do not assume that everyone else has done the same. Behave with them as they expect you to behave; be sympathetic and do not berate them for their mistaken impressions.

32

SOME PEOPLE ASK PSYCHICS AND astrologers how they ought to behave. You know better than paying attention to such superstitions. But even if predictions of future occurrences are made on a scientific basis, these will at best tell you what is likely to happen and can only advise you on the most prudent course of action. But prudent according to what criterion?

If the prediction concerns externals, remember that they are only preferred or dispreferred and do not define who you are. So whether events unfold favorably or unfavorably, the most important things about you are still not affected, and what remains up to you is to react in the best way to whatever happens.

Moreover, if it turns out to be prudent—according to prediction—to act in a way contrary to virtue, to betray a friend's trust, or some such thing, you should react to the prediction as Socrates would, saying that it does not matter, because it is your duty to act virtuously, regardless of whether your actions will turn out to your advantage or not.

33

YOU NEED TO DECIDE WHAT kind of person you are, and then be that person regardless of whether you are in public—with others watching—or in the privacy of your home. Otherwise, you will do a twofold damage to yourself: you will be a hypocrite and, because of your inconsistency, you will make it more difficult for yourself to make progress.

Here are some suggestions concerning the kind of person you may want to be. Don't talk too much; use some time to listen to others instead. After all, you have one mouth and two ears, so perhaps you should train yourself to listen twice as long as you speak. When you do speak, express yourself well and concisely. Try to minimize small talk, you know, about sports, celebrities, or food. That sort of talk doesn't improve you (or others) as a human being. Most importantly, don't talk about other people behind their back, whether it is to blame them, praise them, or compare them to others. If at all possible, attempt to steer the conversation toward meaningful topics. But also remember: you always have the option to remain silent.

Be of good humor, but refrain from laughing too much or too noisily. You are not a child anymore, so be mindful of your dignity.

Refuse, whenever possible, to take oaths. You need to re-serve for yourself the option to arrive at your own judgment about things, and not be bound to blindly follow what others arbitrarily seek to impose on you.

Be mindful of the sort of company you keep. You do not have to accept invitations that put you in association with people who are not interested in bettering themselves. But if it is inevitable that you accept some such invitation, then be careful not to let yourself be steered toward their behavior, if you judge that it is not good for you. Just as your parents told you when you were a kid, the company you keep will stain your soul, for worse or for better. So why would you stain it badly on purpose?

Do not indulge in luxuries. Do take care of your body, your health, and your safety, but try to adopt a rather min-imalist style of life. Luxuries are not only unnecessary, they will easily corrupt you and steer you away from virtue. And if you are tempted to show off some of your possessions to impress others, you are walking on the wrong path, because you still think other people's praise or admiration is a good.

In your sex life, seek pleasure within a committed rela-tionship, so as not to use others and yourself as a means to an end. Never hurt anyone in order to pursue your pleasure. That said, if others indulge in ways that you do not approve of, do not criticize them, and do not flaunt your own example. You don't know why they do what they do, and in any case, their choices are not up to you.

Let's say they tell you that someone has been criticizing you without your knowledge. Instead of defending yourself, say something along the lines of, "Oh, yes, but that's because he doesn't know me well, otherwise he would have much worse to say about me!" Better yet, do not say anything, and ignore the issue. It is nothing to you.

It really isn't necessary to attend sports events. But if you must, train yourself to wish that the team that actually wins be the winner, either because they are the best, or because they are favored by Fortune. Accept the defeat of the opposing team as a fact of life, and as nothing that concerns your progress, because their winning or losing is not up to you. During the event, don't shout or get too excited. Instead, consider the source of your excitement and you will see that it is not worthy of such a response. Finally, don't talk at length about the event after it has happened. It's just not that important.

When you go to any kind of public gathering, remember to maintain your dignity, and strive to never make yourself disagreeable to others.

Suppose you set out to meet a powerful or famous person. Ask yourself the question, "How would Socrates handle this?" And then you'll have a good idea of how to behave. Also, before setting out for the meeting, imagine that you will actually not find them there, or that they will refuse to see you, or that they will treat you rudely. Despite these possibilities, if it is important that you go, then go, and never say "it wasn't worth it," because that's the talk of people who still think that externals are important.

When you are engaged in conversation, make a point of not talking too much about yourself. Hard as it is to believe, you are not as fascinating as you may think, and others are not as interested in you either.

Do not engage in boisterous behavior, and do not use foul language. There is no need, and they tend to bring the conversation down. If other people do such things, it may not be appropriate for you to reproach them directly, but you may do so by refusing to participate in their behavior. Seek virtuous company, and be virtuous company.

34

WHENEVER YOU GET A STRONG impression that some pleasure you should not indulge in would be good for you, slow down, take your time. Distance yourself from the impression; allow it to be carefully considered by your ruling faculty.

In particular, think about how short the time of the actual pleasure will be, and contrast it with how long your regret will last afterward.

Moreover, think of what a different and more refined pleasure you will experience, knowing that you have countered the impression, conquered the desire, and kept your ways virtuous.

IF YOU HAVE DECIDED THAT to do a certain thing is right, do it in full view of others, even though they may disapprove. Their opinion is not up to you.

But if something is not right, then simply don't do it, regardless of what others want you to do. Their opinion is none of your concern.

36

Consider these two sentences: "it is day"; "it is night." Taken separately, each makes sense, and each is true at particular times. But when taken together as one, "it is day and it is night," the sentence entails a contradiction.

Similarly with things that may be good for you and yet not good for the social well-being. They generate another kind of contradiction. For instance, generally speaking, eating whatever you need to nourish your body is preferable. But if you are at someone else's house, you want to be mindful of sharing the food with your host and the other guests, even if you get less than you desire. "Eat what you like" and "share the food socially" are in tension with each other.

So in many other things in life: always wisely consider the trade-offs and balance your own needs with the needs of others.

WE ALL PLAY SEVERAL ROLES in life. But suppose you have decided to play a role that is not appropriate for you, or beyond your abilities. If you were an actor, you would have ruined the play for the spectators, the other actors, and yourself.

So consider carefully what projects you engage in and whether you are suitable for them, and by the same token be sure not to neglect some other projects for which you are, in fact, well suited.

38

I ASSUME THAT YOU ARE careful, in everything you do, not to hurt yourself or, to be specific, your body. You don't go around being careless about nails getting into your shoes, and you walk in such a way as not to sprain your ankle.

So why are you so careless about your ruling faculty? Why do you let it be offended and polluted by all sorts of garbage, instead of guarding it against assaults from without, and taking care from within to sharpen it as much as possible?

EACH PERSON'S BODY IS THE right measure for their property, just like one's foot is the right measure for one's shoes.

What you need are comfortable and durable shoes. But once you pass that mark and start looking for luxury and extravagance, there will be no limit, and your foot will no longer be the measure of your shoe.

The same with body and property. You should have the amount of property, and the size of a dwelling, that is commensurate with the comforts and security of a human being. Once you start going beyond that, there will be no limit, because you will have no right measure to refer things to.

40

THIS SHOULD NOT NEED TO be said, but here it is: people of all genders and ethnicities are fellow human beings, full members of the species, endowed with the same mental potential and intrinsic dignity as all others.

This means that you should treat them the same under all circumstances, whether they happen to be family, lovers, friends, coworkers, or strangers. Discrimination in any measure is never reasonable or virtuous.

IT IS THE MARK OF a person who is not too concerned with virtue to indulge in physical pleasures, too much sex, too much preoccupation with care of the body (including obsessive exercise), and too much eating or drinking, with the resulting undesirable physiological effects.

These are all things to be done with moderation and in a way that does not distract you from cultivating your ruling faculty, the good functioning of which is far more important to you as a human being than all the rest.

II.4

TRAINING YOURSELF TO THINK BETTER

WHERE YOU PREPARE YOURSELF TO IMPROVE
YOUR JUDGMENTS ABOUT THINGS AND PEOPLE

42

If someone speaks badly of you, or does not treat you right, pause and consider why this is the case.

Put yourself in their frame of mind. Presumably, they are convinced that they have good reasons to do what they are doing or say what they are saying. Sure, they may be wrong, but have you not been wrong before? Can you not understand where they are coming from? At any rate, who, exactly is going to be hurt by this?

Consider an example: Imagine someone insists that the square root of nine is four. Is he wrong? Yes. Does that affect the reputation of the square root operation? No. The operation remains untouched, whereas the person who is in error comes across as a fool.

Similarly, if someone speaks badly about you, or does not treat you right, you are not the one who suffers, unless you allow it. Whoever is mistreating you is at fault and worse off for it. If you keep this in mind, then, you will be able to be gentle with those who do wrong and try to correct them. And if they cannot be corrected, you will be more able to generously endure them.

In all such occasions, repeat to yourself, "That's their opinion, and they think they are right."

EVERYTHING HAS TWO HANDLES, METAPHORICALLY speaking. But the two handles are not symmetrical: one makes it easier, the other more difficult, to pick up the thing.

For instance, a family member, or a close friend, has done something to you that you don't think is right. Perhaps they did wrong you. Now, you could use the difficult handle, and cling to the impression that you have been mistreated. This comes naturally, but you are not likely to make much progress that way.

Or, you could pick up the impression with the easier handle, and remember that they are your family or friends, that you have grown up together and share many memories, that they love you and you love them.

Don't you think this would be easier, and moreover better for the long run?

44

HERE ARE SOME COMMON ATTITUDES that make no logical sense: "I am richer than you, therefore a better person." Or: "I am better educated than you, therefore a better person." The conclusion simply does not follow from the premise.

What does follow? "I am richer than you, therefore I have more money." Or: "I am better educated than you, therefore I can speak better."

But you are neither money nor speech. You are a person capable of making decisions. And it is only by the quality of those decisions that you ought to be judged, or to judge yourself.

Don't say that someone drinks too much, only say that someone is drinking. Don't say that someone talks too much, only say that someone is talking.

Generally speaking, you simply do not know enough about other people, and why they do what they do, to arrive at secure judgments about them. Maybe that would be too much drinking or talking *for you*, but how do you know the same goes for them?

Remember that your goal should be to arrive at the best possible judgments about things and people, and that will not happen if you rush into it without sufficient information and deliberation. Most of the time, simply abstaining from judgment will actually be the better course.

TRAINING TO LIVE WELL

WHERE YOU PREPARE YOURSELF TO PRACTICE
THE ART OF LIVING

46

DON'T EVEN THINK OF CALLING yourself wise, or enlightened, or whatever. To be ostentatious is a sure mark that you are not, in fact, wise or enlightened. Instead of pontificating, *act* according to what you've learned. That will be far more impressive.

For instance, let's say that you are at a dinner party. Don't lecture others about how people ought to eat. Just eat properly. Socrates famously admitted that he was not wise and did not know much. Are you any better than Socrates? He didn't mind being overlooked on account of his humble appearance, because he knew that appearances are not a good measure of a person. Are you more in need or more deserving of attention than Socrates?

Let me put it another way. When sheep eat their food, do they regurgitate it in front of the shepherd so to gloat and be praised? No, they take their time to digest it, in order to slowly transform it into wool and milk. *That* is what is valuable for the shepherd.

The same goes for you: Be careful not to vomit in front of others some undigested principles, just so that you can impress people. Instead, digest those principles slowly and surely, so that they may result in what really matters: better behavior on your part.

47

HERE IS HOW TO PRACTICE excellence at being human: on your own, without showy displays of virtue to others.

Did you decide that a simple diet with less impact on the environment and less suffering imposed on animals is preferable? Excellent. So eat that way, without feeling the need to explain to others why you do so. They'll see it with their own eyes.

Did you decide that drinking alcohol is not appropriate for you? Very well, then, don't drink it. Do not make a display of it to others just so they can praise you.

Did you decide that you need to work out to make your body healthier and stronger? Good for you. No need to share that with the whole world so that people will be impressed.

Do you want to practice endurance? Here is a simple way to do it: Next time you are thirsty, take some cold water into your mouth, then spit it out. But without telling anyone.

48

HERE IS THE BASIC DIFFERENCE between those who practice the art of living and those who don't. The latter look to externals, like money, property, and reputation for comfort, and blame those same things when harmed. Practitioners, by contrast, look at themselves for both comfort and the source of harm.

Here are some sure signs that someone is making progress in their practice: They don't criticize anyone, they don't praise anyone, they don't blame anyone, they find fault with no one, and never refer to themselves as being somebody or knowing something. When they are hindered, they look at what incorrect judgment they may have made. When someone compliments them, they smile to themselves instead of feeling flattered; when someone criticizes them, they accept the criticism in good spirit.

In other words, practicing the art of living means going about in life as if we were recovering from an illness, protecting and nursing the injured parts so that they can recover properly. We are learning what is proper to desire and what is proper to avoid or no longer desire, which turns out to be quite different from what most people put into those categories.

We abstain from judgment as much as it is possible, conscious of the fact that we don't really know much. If in so doing we appear foolish or ignorant, we do not care. Above all, we keep guard against our own foolishness, as if it were an enemy lying in wait, ready to ambush us.

49

So you are proud of having gotten into philosophy, right? Are you assuming the air of someone who knows things with your friends and acquaintances? But what is it, exactly, that you know? You have read Socrates and Epictetus, maybe you understand what they are saying. But are you actually living like them? Does your interpretation of philosophical texts lead you to live a better life? If not, you are no different from someone who can read Homer or Shakespeare and talk about them in an abstruse manner, but who couldn't write a paragraph to save their life!

The only thing to be proud of is your practice, day after day. It is only when you can actually live these precepts, and not just read or talk about them, that you can call yourself a person who is earnestly practicing the art of living. And that definitely is something to be proud of!

50

YOU SHOULDN'T JUST MEMORIZE THESE principles, but follow them every day, as if they were laws of nature. Though keep in mind that, so far as we can tell, there is no law giver or immutable cosmic essence. Rather, what you have been learning is the result of human wisdom that originated from, and has been applied to, the human condition.

Moreover, remember not to pay attention to those who criticize or belittle you—unless you can learn from them. Their opinions are not up to you. Only your own judgment is.

51

WHY ARE YOU STILL WAITING to be the best that you can be? You have heard the message, you have understood it, and you have agreed with it. So, what's stopping you from putting it into practice?

Are you still waiting for the right teacher, the right guide? But they have already arrived, haven't you noticed? You are not a child anymore, you are an adult. You have no time left for being neglectful and easygoing, for furthering delay, or for coming up with additional excuses or needing to do this, that, or the other before you finally turn your attention to yourself and to your own improvement.

If you don't pay attention, you will continue to live mindlessly, never embracing and practicing the art of living. You will make no progress, and you will die that way. What a shame.

Get on with the program, then! Make up your mind to do what must be done. The right thing to do is to live as a human being—which means as one who uses the faculty of reason to improve society—and to focus on what is best and stay with it.

Think of your philosophical training as a contest, as if you were at the Olympic games. Haven't you noticed? They have already started! It isn't possible to delay any longer, to keep mulling things over. You must act now, or progress will be lost and you will have to start afresh.

This is how Socrates came to be who he was, by paying attention to nothing but his reason while working for others. Perhaps you are no Socrates, but you ought to live as one who wishes to be Socrates.

52

THERE ARE THREE DIVISIONS OF practical philosophy. The first division has to do with what to do or not to do. For instance, don't lie (other things being equal). The second division deals with knowing why certain precepts are valid or not. For instance, why shouldn't I lie (in this case, given these circumstances)? The third division refines the first two by adding layers of insight and understanding. For instance, is this reason for not lying a good one? Does it stand up to scrutiny? What is the difference between truth and lie? And so on.

In a sense, the third division is necessary as a result of the second, and the second as a result of the first. But the first division is obviously the most important, because if we discern what to do and why, and yet fail to do it, then what is any of this good for?

The problem is that people tend to invert the priority, thinking that the third division is most important, while gingerly neglecting the first one. As a result, we lie at the very same time as we have at the ready arguments for why others ought not to lie.

II.6

FOUR PIECES OF ADVICE FROM EPICTETUS

WHERE WE LISTEN TO THE MASTER

53

I. What decides whether a sum of money is good? The money is not going to tell you; it must be the faculty that makes use of such impressions—reason. (*Discourses* I, 1.5)

II. Whenever externals are more important to you than your own integrity, then be prepared to serve them for the remainder of your life. (*Discourses* II, 2.12)

III. Speaking for myself, I hope death overtakes me when I'm occupied solely with the care of my character, in an effort to make it undisturbed, free, unrestricted and unrestrained. (*Discourses* III, 5.7)

IV. The more we value things outside of our control, the less control we have. (*Discourses* IV, 4.23)

PART III

STOICISM 2.0

UPDATING STOICISM

All philosophies of life and religions (which are a kind of philosophy of life) change over time. Change is inevitable. The only difference is that some people agree to change reluctantly, while others believe change is necessary for a philosophy of life to remain relevant. The Stoics clearly belonged to the second category, as Seneca actually explicitly says in his thirty-third letter to his friend Lucilius:

> Will I not walk in the footsteps of my predecessors? I will indeed use the ancient road—but if I find another route that is more direct and has fewer ups and downs, I will stake out that one. Those who advanced these doctrines before us are not our masters but our guides. The truth lies open to all; it

has not yet been taken over. Much is left also for those yet to come.[1]

I think the best way to approach my proposal for a Stoicism 2.0, so to speak, is to go back to the classic distinctions the Stoics themselves made among what they called the three parts of philosophy: "logic," "physics," and "ethics." I will explain why I employ the scare quotes around these terms in a minute. Here is how Diogenes Laertius summarizes the original Stoic take:

> Philosophic doctrine, say the Stoics, falls into three parts: one physical, another ethical, and the third logical. . . . Philosophy, they say, is like an animal, Logic corresponding to the bones and sinews, Ethics to the fleshy parts, Physics to the soul. Another simile they use is that of an egg: the shell is Logic, next comes the white, Ethics, and the yolk in the centre is Physics. Or, again, they liken Philosophy to a fertile field: Logic being the encircling fence, Ethics the crop, Physics the soil or the trees. Or, again, to a city strongly walled and governed by reason.[2]

Of the above potpourri of metaphors, my preferred one is that of the fertile field, because it gets things in what I think is the right order. The fundamental idea is that good reasoning reduces our chances to commit blunders, which is why

Logic is represented by the fence that protects the field. But in order to get a good crop (Ethics)—which is the ultimate goal—one also needs nutritious soil, represented here by the Physics. Why? Because it is hard to live well if one maintains radical misconceptions about how the world works.

What would a badly fenced and infertile field look like? Suppose you believe in the Law of Attraction, a pseudoscientific notion made popular by the book *The Secret*. Then you also believe that the universe will somehow reconfigure itself to accommodate your wishes, if only your wishes are strong and sincere enough. That means that you are not reasoning well, and that you profoundly misunderstand how the universe actually works.

In a sense, then, the Stoic philosophical recipe boils down to this equation:

Logic + Physics = Ethics

We must, however, keep in mind a simple but important caveat: the words "logic," "physics," and "ethics" are defined by the Stoics, and indeed by most ancient philosophers, far more broadly than implied by the modern meaning of those terms. As should be clear by now, "logic" in this sense includes anything that improves our reasoning: not only formal logic, but also cognitive science, an awareness of fallacies and biases, and even dialectics (the ability to engage in constructive dialogue with others). "Physics" really means the totality of the natural sciences (not just physics in the narrow sense, but also biology, geology, astronomy, chemistry, etc.), as well as metaphysics (the branch of philosophy that is in the business of making sense of the overall picture of the world emerging from the individual sciences). Finally, "ethics" isn't just the study of right and wrong, as the word is often narrowly used nowadays, but nothing less than the study of how to live our life.

So even though I am proposing changes to what Epictetus has taught, I have still sought to derive them by the same general philosophical method used by the Stoics. My version of Stoicism 2.0 hinges on seven themes where my take differs more or less significantly from Epictetus's. These themes are explored in what follows, in order of first appearance of each theme in the *Enchiridion* / Field Guide. The first appendix to this book then includes a table listing every major change I have made, by way of a direct, section-by-section comparison between the *Enchiridion* and the Field Guide. This will be useful to readers who wish to have a detailed understanding of my proposal.

THEME 1: EXTERNALS DON'T NEED TO BE DESPISED

While the notion that Stoics go through life with a stiff upper lip is a misguided stereotype, there is a grain of truth in it, since endurance of adverse conditions certainly is a Stoic value. But Epictetus, and even Seneca—who was in some sense the most humane of the Stoics—often go further and openly encourage us to despise "externals," that is, things like health, wealth, reputation, and so forth. This stems from the fundamental Stoic doctrine that virtue is the only good and everything else is a "preferred indifferent," meaning that it may be reasonably selected, so long as this doesn't compromise one's moral character.

Socrates, who formulated an early version of this idea, makes an argument for what later became the Stoic position in the dialogue known as the Euthydemus, where he confronts two Sophists, the title character and his brother, Dionysodorus. One of the crucial points of the dialogue (279–282) is Socrates's encomium of wisdom, where he explains that wisdom is all that matters because wise people do well and prosper in anything they do. Happiness, he claims, doesn't derive from having goods or knowledge, but from using goods and knowledge wisely. Socrates goes even so far as to suggest that if one is not wise, one is better off without goods or knowledge, because he risks using them unwisely, which is worse than not having them at all.

Notice, however, that the Socratic position does not entail that externals need to be despised, nor is there any reason why one should cultivate virtue (or wisdom) to the complete exclusion of externals. Socrates certainly didn't do it, and to adopt such an extreme take is really to embrace the Cynic philosophy embodied by the flamboyant Diogenes of Sinope—whom Plato famously referred to as "Socrates gone mad."

Indeed, Socrates makes clear that one cannot exercise virtue *without* engaging with externals. A person is wise or virtuous (I am, you may have noticed, using the two terms interchangeably) precisely in direct proportion to how well she makes use of externals.

A good way to make sense of what I'm proposing is to think in terms of what modern economists call lexicographic preferences. Behavioral economists have realized that—contra classical economic theory—people don't consider all goods or desiderata to be fungible, that is interchangeable, for a given good or desideratum of equal economic value. Rather, people group the things they want or care for into separate sets, and order the sets according to their importance. While members of the same set can be traded against each other, members of different sets usually aren't.

Let me give you a concrete example. In the realm of ordinary life, my "A-set" includes, for instance, my daughter. I care for her welfare, her future, and so forth. My "B-set" includes an orange Lamborghini, my ideal car. Now, I would be perfectly willing—if I could afford it—to trade a lot of cash (which also belongs to the B-set) for a Lamborghini. But trading my daughter's welfare or future for the car is simply completely out of the question.

Similarly, I think that modern Stoics should consider virtue as the only item worthy of belonging to the A-set, and of externals as ranked in a series of lower sets of importance. Here, my daughter then shifts to the B-set, and the Lamborghini to the C-set. Virtue is still the highest good, and moreover it is in a category of its own, and cannot be traded for anything else. But externals are also goods (of a lower rank), and it makes no sense to despise or avoid them. In fact, they are the indispensable raw material on which we exercise our virtue. Virtue cannot be cultivated in a vacuum, after all.

Yet another way to put the point, which makes sense of the deliciously oxymoronic phrase often used in both ancient and modern Stoicism, "preferred indifferents," is that having certain externals (say, being wealthy) doesn't make you a good person, nor does lacking them (say, being poor) make you a bad person. Therefore, items that fall into the B-set and lower logically remain separate and independent of the only thing that qualifies for the A-set: virtue.

THEME 2: NO NEED TO CULTIVATE INDIFFERENCE TO HUMAN LOSS

For most people who approach Epictetus for the first time, by far the hardest bit to swallow is *Enchiridion* 3. W. A. Oldfather's 1925 translation goes like this:

With everything which entertains you, is useful, or of which you are fond, remember to say to yourself, beginning with the very least things, 'What is its nature?' If you are fond of a jug, say, 'I am fond of a jug'; for when it is broken you will not be disturbed. If you kiss your own child or wife, say to yourself that you are kissing a human being; for when it dies you will not be disturbed.

It may be tempting to attribute the apparent callousness of the last bit to an inaccurate translation. But the original Greek is just as harsh. Epictetus himself appeared to have been a nice chap, so the passage (and several others, in both the *Enchiridion* and the *Discourses*) is not *meant* to be callous. The author is simply stating what he sees as a combination of a fact of nature ("physics": people are mortal, including our loved ones) and of sound reasoning ("logic": it makes no sense to be distraught by inevitable facts). Despite their internal consistency, passages such as this one give Stoics the reputation for being people who seek to suppress all emotions.

The fact is, Epictetus had the advantage of believing in a kind of cosmic Providence, which could afford him that sort of detachment—similar to the notion of nonattachment in Buddhism, which leans on that religion's belief in karma and reincarnation. The problem is that the modern scientific outlook is not compatible with the ancient Stoics' take on how the world works (more on this when we discuss theme 5), and so we are left to face our own reality in which there is a significant difference between the breaking of a cup and the dying of a child or partner.

Still, modern Stoics can retain much of the original insight, not by treating the breaking of a mug in the same fashion as the death of a loved one, but by training themselves to accept inevitable events with magnanimity (literally, in Greek, greatness of soul). What I am suggesting is something akin to a memorable scene from the movie *Bridge of Spies*. The two major characters in the story are lawyer James Donovan and accused Russian spy Rudolf Abel. During Abel's trial for treason, Donovan notices that his client doesn't seem disturbed by the very real possibility of facing the death penalty. So at one point he asks Abel, "Aren't you worried?" Abel's response is, "Would it help?" This reaction does not imply that Abel likes the idea of dying on the electric chair, but rather that he has developed a remarkable attitude of simultaneous acceptance of the inevitable and the ability to direct his focus on where he can actually act, here and now, during the trial. Exactly like the dichotomy of control says we should.

THEME 3: LIVE ACCORDING TO NATURE

Diogenes Laertius explains what the ancient Stoics meant by their catchphrase, "live according to nature":

This is why Zeno was the first (in his treatise On the Nature of Man) to designate as the end "life in agreement with nature" (or living agreeably to nature), which is the same as a virtuous life, virtue being the goal towards which nature guides us. So too Cleanthes in his treatise On Pleasure, as also Posidonius, and Hecato in his work On Ends. Again, living virtuously is equivalent to living in accordance with experience of the actual course of nature, as Chrysippus says in the first book of his De finibus; for our individual natures are parts of the nature of the whole universe. And this is why the end may be defined as life in accordance with nature, or, in other words, in accordance with our own human nature as well as that of the universe.[3]

This is another bit of ancient Stoicism that derives its immediate sense from the concept of a providential cosmos, which, again, is untenable in the light of modern science. But our evolving knowledge of the cosmos does not mean that we should do away with the whole notion of living according to nature, only that we should properly reinterpret what such a directive means.

In fact, we can maintain the same dual interpretation that Chrysippus proposes, but from a different perspective. To live according to cosmic nature, in modern terms, just means to accept the world for what it is, as distinct from what we would like it to be. Or, as modern Stoic Larry Becker puts it,[4] "follow the facts" (of physics and biology). To live according to human nature, by contrast, can pretty much still be interpreted as the ancient Stoics did, since their notion that human beings are fundamentally social and capable of reason is certainly confirmed by modern primatology, anthropology, and cognitive science.

So when Epictetus says that we should go to the baths,[5] for instance, having two goals in mind: to enjoy ourselves and to keep harmony with nature, we can rephrase it as to enjoy ourselves and to remain reasonable and pro-social (i.e., not getting angry with fellow human beings). As he points out, correctly, the first is not up to us, because it depends on circumstances and other people. But the second one certainly is.

THEME 4: QUESTIONABLE SCIENCE OR METAPHYSICS

The ancient Stoics believed in a number of notions that we consider pseudoscientific, most famously divination.[6] Epictetus explicitly mentions the practice—taking it for granted—at *Enchiridion* 18 and 32, for instance. This belief was not as far-fetched as it may seem. The Stoics thought that all events are connected to each other via a universal web of cause-effect, just like modern scientists do. From this premise, it then stands to reason that it should be possible to predict (i.e., "divine") future events based on reasoned analysis of the present state of the cosmos. Modern physics works by the same logic, with the substantial difference that the Stoics were at least some of the time focusing on the wrong (because uninformative) causal connections, or considered to be causal some connections that were actually inert (with respect to predicting the future), such as animal entrails, for instance.

Nothing of substance is lost for modern Stoics if we simply identify any untenable (by modern standards) bit of ancient Stoic metaphysics and either discard it or update it by using the best science available to us. Of course, modern Stoics and scientists such as myself readily acknowledge that our current knowledge too will eventually be replaced by even more advanced knowledge. As the history of Stoicism demonstrates, we have not reached the end point, and we probably never will.

THEME 5: GOD OR ATOMS

This is perhaps the most radical change I am proposing to Stoicism 1.0, and it is already creating controversy among Stoics in both scholarly and public circles. For this reason, I must be clear on what exactly I am suggesting and why.

The ancient Stoics were pantheists;[7] that is, they believed that God was immanent in the cosmos and coincident with nature. Again, Diogenes Laertius:

> God is one and the same with Reason, Fate, and Zeus; he is also called by many other names. . . . The term universe

or cosmos is used by them in three senses: (1) of God himself . . . (2) Again, they give the name of cosmos to the orderly arrangement of the heavenly bodies in itself as such; and (3) in the third place to that whole of which these two are parts.[8]

The idea was that the cosmos is permeated by a single substance, the *pneuma* (literally, breath), which has different manifestations depending on its "tension." The lowest grade is common to everything, including inanimate objects; the middle grade is what distinguishes living organisms; and the highest grade, the *logos*, is present only in organisms capable of reason. This latter category includes only the universe as a whole (conceived as a sentient living organism), and of course human beings, who are literally bits and pieces of that cosmic organism.

From this understanding, the Stoics derived their concept of Providence. Epictetus uses the metaphor of a foot stepping into the mud,[9] observing that the foot isn't going to like getting dirty, but if it realized that it is connected to a living body, which has to cross a muddy street to get home, then the foot would be glad to do its part. Analogously, we should be glad of (and embrace, not just accept) whatever happens to us because it is for the good of the universe.

Notice that this is very different from the standard Christian conception of Providence. In the latter case, God actually cares for and loves every single one of us, even though God's plans may be inscrutable to us. What Epictetus and the Stoics conjure is a picture of an organ (a foot, or maybe even just an epithelial cell) that does what it does for the benefit of the whole organism. The organ doesn't have a choice in the matter, and the organism doesn't care about the fate of individual organs (or cells).

I find the Stoic notion of Providence beautiful and comforting. But as a scientist living in the twenty-first century, I cannot accept it. We have no reason to believe that sentience is a property of the cosmos (except in the trivial sense that the cosmos contains sentient organisms—us). Or that there is any such thing as the *pneuma* or similar all-permeating substance. Or that the universe is in any way like a living organism.[10]

Why did the Stoics think this was so? Essentially, they deployed what in philosophy is known as the argument from intelligent design,[11] as Epictetus does here:

Who is it that has fitted the sword to the scabbard and the scabbard to the sword? Is there no one? Surely the very structure of such finished products leads us commonly to infer that they must be the work of some craftsman, and are not constructed at random. Are we to say then that each of these products points to the craftsman, but that things visible and vision and light do not? Do not male and female and the desire of union and the power to use the organs adapted for it—do not these point to the craftsman?[12]

No, they don't, though it was reasonable to think so in Epictetus's time. As I explain in chapter 6 of my *How to Be a Stoic*, David Hume (1711–1776) and Charles Darwin (1809–1882) dealt a fatal double blow to the intelligent design argument, a blow from which the argument never recovered—philosophically or scientifically.

But why abide by whatever modern science says, especially since scientists keep proposing new theories all the time? Simply because science is by far the best (indeed, pretty much the only) approach we have devised to investigate the world around us. Scientists make mistakes. They are biased by their own ideological preconceptions, and they are just as greedy and selfish (or generous and altruistic) as any other human being. But there simply is no other game in town, when it comes to understanding the reality of which we are a part.

Grasping that reality used to be the primary objective of so-called first philosophy, or metaphysics. For centuries philosophers (who, until the late eighteenth century, were not actually distinct from scientists) pursued the goal of discovering truths about reality by way of a priori, logical arguments. The last great attempt in that direction was done by René Descartes (he of the famous "I think therefore I am") in the seventeenth century, and it failed. Science, as we understand it today, was born at about the same time (Descartes was a contemporary of Galileo).

Nowadays, metaphysicians are split into two camps: those who still think we can do first philosophy, and those espousing so-called scientific metaphysics.[13] My opinion is that the original approach is now dead in the water, having been replaced by the natural sciences. (Just ask yourself, how many new discoveries have metaphysicians made in the last, oh, I don't know, five centuries?) The second one, however, plays a crucial role in both philosophy and science, since the goal of scientific metaphysics is to make overall sense of the disparate bits and pieces of knowledge about the world coming from the "special" sciences (e.g., physics, chemistry, biology, geology, psychology, and so forth). This is obviously important, and not a task for which scientists are well suited, for the simple reason that modern science is highly specialized, and no practicing scientist can develop the necessary breadth of knowledge. (Philosophers can, because they don't have to carry out costly and highly specific empirical research.)

All of the above just to make the point that my rejection of this bit of Stoic metaphysics in favor of modern science is neither arbitrary nor unfounded. Nor is it without respect for those such as Epictetus who were doing the best they could with the knowledge available in their time.

There are two more, crucial, aspects that I want to discuss with regard to metaphysics and Stoicism. First, despite my rejection of the notion of a sentient cosmos, a lot of Stoic metaphysics is here to stay, and I think that those that survive are the most important parts. The Stoics were materialists, thinking that the world is made of stuff, with no supernatural or immaterial entities. Even God itself, and the human soul, were made of stuff for them. This is in synch with the modern scientific outlook, where "stuff" is whatever contemporary physics tells us are the most fundamental constituents of the universe (quarks, strings, fields, or whatnot). As we have seen, the Stoics also thought that everything is connected by a universal web of cause-effect, which again is in agreement with science as it has been practiced since Galileo. These two points are crucial because a number of consequences for Stoic ethics follow from them, arguably the most important of which is the dichotomy of control. And remember, the dichotomy of control is where the *Enchiridion* and this Field Guide begin.

Second, even though I think the most reasonable take on Stoic metaphysics is the one that I have just outlined, this doesn't preclude people who espouse different metaphysics (up to a point) from embracing and practicing Stoicism. Stoic philosophy is rather ecumenical, in this respect, and Stoicism offers a wide tent that can welcome a variety of ideological commitments, including religious-metaphysical and even, again up to a point, political ones.

Modern Stoics can easily be pantheists, just like the ancient ones. Or, they can interpret the Logos as Christians do, as the word of God. Each interpretation comes with its own set of internal tensions, which individual practitioners will have to resolve in whatever way makes the most sense to them. Not *every* metaphysical position is compatible with Stoicism (the Law of Attraction, mentioned above, is one that is not), but several are, and my take is by no means the only one on the table.[14]

THEME 6: LOCAL CUSTOMS ARE NEITHER UNIVERSAL NOR IMMUTABLE

Epictetus was alive between the end of the first and the beginning of the second century. And he was not omniscient, which means that—like the rest of us—he was a man of his time and place. What is valuable about his philosophy are the universal ideas that it contains about human nature, not the specific notions he endorsed or took for granted because he happened to be a Roman citizen during the Empire.

But limitations of time and place are precisely why we need to reconsider some of Epictetus's examples, and even some of his specific ethical injunctions. For instance, he often talks of slavery (remember, he was a slave himself!), as if that institution were part of normal life.[15] During the Roman

Empire, slavery was indeed part of daily life, and in fact the entire economy of the Empire was based on it. But it should go without saying that we now know better. Or consider his assumption that it is okay for a father to strike a son.[16] It is not, by very recent modern standards. Lastly, there is the injunction that sexual relations should be "pure" and limited to marriage and procreation,[17] a position that is unnecessarily restrictive for people of all genders and sexual orientations in today's society.

When Epictetus deploys his theory of role ethics, that is, the notion that we find guidance in how to behave by considering the various roles we play in society, such as father, daughter, friend, colleague, and so forth, he is obviously referring to the understanding of those roles typical of his own time and culture. But humanity has made moral progress over the past two millennia,[18] and hopefully will continue to do so in the future. Which means that how these very same roles are understood and interpreted is in constant flux.

However, this acknowledgment of cultural progression does not alter the substance of Epictetus's advice—say, that we should be respectful of our parents and that who they are or how they act toward us is not under our control. We moderns just maintain that this advice does not imply that we should submit to physical or psychological abuse, even from our parents. The point is more important than it may seem at first, because there may be legitimate doubt or confusion about what is actually logically entailed by Stoic philosophy apart from what is rooted in the customs of the time. A good example is the issue of feminism, which pertains to the next theme, that of social justice.

The term "social justice" is, nowadays, surprisingly controversial. So, let me clarify what I mean when I use it in this context. The ancient Stoics were remarkably ahead of their time in terms of how they thought of women and slaves. Seneca, for instance, writes to his friend Marcia in the first century of the current era that women have the same analytical capacities as men, which meant that they had the ability to study and practice philosophy.[19] And he very clearly states that slaves are human beings like any other, and ought to be treated accordingly.[20] Zeno, the founder of Stoicism, went so far as to label slavery an evil already in the fourth century BCE.[21] As for racism, the ancient Greco-Romans simply did not think of races as we understand the concept in contemporary discourse. Our discussions of race are rooted in the so-called scientific racism developed during the Enlightenment and brutally applied during colonialism. For the Greco-Romans, slaves (when they were not born that way) were previously free individuals who happened to have lost in battle—something that could just as easily happen, and did happen, repeatedly, to the Greeks and Romans themselves.

Still, even a superficial reading of Seneca or Epictetus will make modern readers cringe, given how their writings are freely peppered with demeaning comments toward women, who are often used to represent the paragon of emotional weakness. The thing is, as modern scholars have argued in detail,[22] there is no reason whatsoever within Stoicism to discriminate on the basis of sex, gender, ethnicity, or any other arbitrary or biological categorization of human beings. On the contrary, the fundamental Stoic notion of cosmopolitanism[23] entails that any such discrimination ought to be rejected as incompatible with Stoic philosophy. Hence my rephrasing of pertinent bits of Epictetus.

ᔥ III.2 ᔥ

THIS IS NOT THE
FIRST TIME, AND IT
WON'T BE THE LAST

I am most certainly not the first to rewrite or update the *Enchiridion*. Nor, doubtlessly, will I be the last. This may sound strange, and even presumptuous of me, but as I have already argued, philosophies of life and religions are not static entities, they evolve over time.

Consider for instance the religion I grew up with in Italy, Roman Catholicism. Very few people in the world, including so-called fundamentalists, would argue that we ought to read the Old and New Testament as if societal norms, and moral norms in particular, had remained unchanged over the last two millennia. That's why there is no such thing as a "literal" reading of Scripture, notwithstanding the loud proclamations of a number of misguided souls. And if we can reasonably reinterpret and update what some refer to as God's own words, surely we can do the same with mortals such as Epictetus. The *Enchiridion*, after all, is not a sacred text.

Like Seneca, I consider Zeno, Epictetus, Marcus Aurelius, and in fact Seneca himself, to be my guides, not my masters. From the onset Stoicism was marked by vibrant discussions not just with rival schools—the Epicureans, the Academic Skeptics, the Peripatetics—but internally. I have already pointed out that Chrysippus made major innovations, in direct disagreement with the first two heads of the Stoa, Zeno and Cleanthes. The middle Stoics Panaetius and Posidonius also explored different directions, some of which were incorporated by successive generations, others rejected. There are limits, of course, to how much one can revise a system of ideas or philosophy. Perhaps the most famous Stoic "heretic" was Aristo of Chios, who flourished around 260 BCE (only four decades after the foundation of the Stoa). He rejected the standard Stoic notion that in order to study ethics we also need logic and physics. The resulting system ended up being very close to that of the Cynics, and Aristo eventually left the Stoa entirely.

Later on, during the Renaissance, Justus Lipsius (1547–1606) attempted a radical update of Stoic philosophy in order to make it overtly compatible with Christianity. His starting point was Seneca, and his work influenced a number of major early modern figures, including Montesquieu, Francis Bacon, Francisco de Quevedo, and Peter Paul Rubens. Eventually Neo-Stoicism, as it was called, was banned by the Church as heretical, and yet both Christianity and Stoicism continued to change and adapt to the times.

The relationship between Christianity and Stoicism, and particularly between Christianity and Epictetus, is complex and fascinating.[1] At least four different versions of the *Enchiridion* were produced in order to train Christian monks, in the tenth, eleventh, fourteenth, and seventeenth centuries. Sometimes the modifications to the original were minor, like substituting Paul (of Tarsus) for Socrates. In other cases they were more substantial, with entire sections omitted or expanded, and new sections added.

The most recent modern rendition of the *Enchiridion* is due to Sharon Lebelle in 1995, under the title *The Art of Living: The Classic Manual on Virtue, Happiness, and Effectiveness*. It is a paraphrase in modern language, not a conceptual update, but it is nevertheless a testament to the continuing fascination that Epictetus exercises over people across cultures and millennia.

Naturally, the question will arise: But is this *still* Stoicism? The answer will depend on the specifics, and will not be satisfactory to everyone. As always, this will be for you to consider and decide. Aristo thought of himself as a Stoic, until he didn't, realizing that his doctrines had veered too far from the original for it to be reasonable to retain the label. Despite the many points in which my Field Guide diverges from Epictetus's *Enchiridion*, I call my philosophy Stoicism because I think it remains true, in most part, to the school founded by Zeno and to the tradition he initiated.

Ultimately, of course, labels don't matter. If you got to this point in the book and think that what I'm proposing is no longer Stoicism, that's okay. The real question, in the end, is this: Is it useful?

By now, I hope that you will see why I was astounded that I never heard of Epictetus before my chance encounter with him several years ago, why I fell in love, so to speak, with his thought and persona, and why I decided to write a book that is both an homage to him and a novel way to introduce new generations to his wisdom, updated to take into account the two millennia that have passed since he lectured to Arrian. It is my ambition that my work will allow several more future generations to benefit from the wisdom of the sage from Hierapolis and of the Stoics more generally.

APPENDIX I

A CONCEPTUAL MAP OF THE DIFFERENCES BETWEEN THE *ENCHIRIDION* AND THE FIELD GUIDE

THIS IS A UNIT-BY-UNIT COMPARISON of the original *Enchiridion* and my Field Guide. If a unit is not explicitly listed, my version is conceptually similar to Epictetus's and requires no special explanation. The first column in the table refers to the numbered unit in the *Enchiridion* / Field Guide; the second column is a summary of Epictetus's take; the third column synthesizes my view; and the last column refers to the general theme to which the change pertains, as explained in the previous section.

Section	Original	New	General Theme
1	No explanation of dichotomy of control. // Have to choose between making progress and acquiring externals. // Impressions of things not up to us should be nothing to us.	Addition of explanation of dichotomy of control, rejection of the (modern) notion of a continuum between control and no control. // Don't have to choose between progress and externals, just acknowledge that initially practice will be difficult. // Impressions of things not up to us may generate preferences, but should not affect self-worth.	Externals don't need to be despised or avoided.
2	Withdraw entirely from externals, at least in the beginning.	Move your goals from external to internal. It is okay to select a certain outcome, so long as one accepts a contrary outcome with equanimity.	Externals don't need to be despised or avoided.
3	Whether it is a mug that breaks or a loved one who dies, you should train yourself not to be disturbed.	Prepare yourself for loss in general, but do not be callous about the loss of human beings. Accepting reality does not mean not caring for people.	No need to cultivate indifference to human loss.
4	No matter what you do, you also want to keep in harmony with the universe.	You want to keep harmony with others and with yourself.	Live according to human nature.
5	Death cannot be bad, or it would have seemed so to Socrates.	Death is not bad because you won't be there when it comes (Epicurean argument). // Irrationality of anti-death cults, religious or technological.	Questionable science or metaphysics.
7	The "Captain" who calls is a metaphor for God.	No need to invoke gods. // Life as a voyage.	God or atoms.

Section	Original	New	General Theme
8	Love whatever happens to you (amor fati, as Nietzsche later put it).	You can't love something that is not the result of a benevolent Providence. But you can accept with equanimity whatever happens, being glad when things go your way, serene when they don't.	No need to cultivate indifference to human loss.
11	Reference to a "Giver" of things, which he then takes back.	No necessary reference to any "Giver," while keeping the metaphor of the inn.	God or atoms.
12	Talk of slavery.	No consideration of slavery as a concept.	Local customs are not universal or immutable.
13	Either pursue externals or make progress.	You can pursue externals, but you need to train yourself to think they are not the most important thing.	Externals don't need to be despised or avoided.
14	Talk of slavery.	No consideration of slavery as a concept.	Local customs are not universal or immutable.
15	Ideally, you should despise externals, not just take them in moderate measure.	No despising required; that is what a Cynic would do, not a Stoic.	Externals don't need to be despised or avoided.
16	Be sympathetic to the problems of others, but remember to not groan inwardly.	Cultivate equanimity toward adversity, yours as well as that of others.	No need to cultivate indifference to human loss.

Section	Original	New	General theme
17	Metaphor of acting in a play refers to the "Playwright," that is, God.	No Playwright is necessary. // A better metaphor for life is that of playing a game of poker.	God or atoms.
18	Don't pay attention to portents, because they can only affect externals.	Don't pay attention to superstition in general, because it is based on a false understanding of how the world works.	Questionable science or metaphysics.
23	You turn either to externals or to philosophy.	Externals have value, but they are not your chief goal.	Externals don't need to be despised or avoided.
26	When your child dies, it is not a catastrophe. // Talk of slavery.	Losing loved ones is painful, but you should keep in mind that it is natural, and it happens to others as well. Develop a sense of equanimity about it. // No consideration of slavery as a concept.	No need to cultivate indifference to human loss. // Local customs are not universal or immutable.
29	Either be a philosopher or pursue externals. // Talk of slavery.	You will not get everything you want in life, and your priority should be to cultivate yourself. // No consideration of slavery as a concept.	Externals don't need to be despised or avoided. // Local customs are not universal or immutable.
30	Submit to your father even if he strikes or abuses you.	Parents should be given respect, but not submission.	Local customs are not universal or immutable.

Section	Original	New	General Theme
31	Mention of gods and piety.	Mention of cosmic web of cause-effect, skepticism of gods.	God or atoms.
32	Mention of divination.	Rejection of any sort of superstition.	Questionable science or metaphysics.
33	Talk of slavery. // Preserving purity in terms of sexual relations.	No consideration of slavery as a concept. // We accept that sexual relations are more varied, fluid, and complex than in Epictetus's time.	Local customs are not universal or immutable.
40	While less than customary by the time, there is a certain degree of sexism.	No sexism, or discrimination against any gender or ethnicity.	Social justice. // Local customs are not universal.
48	The person who makes progress has put away every desire.	The person who makes progress has figured out what is good for them to desire.	Externals don't need to be despised or avoided.
50	Stoic precepts are like laws of nature.	There are—so far as we know—no laws of ethics, no law giver, no cosmic essence. Only human wisdom and experience.	God or atoms.
53	Talk of divinity, mention of the famous "Hymn to Zeus" by Cleanthes.	No gods or prayers, just good old Epictetean common sense.	God or atoms.

APPENDIX II

A REASONED BIBLIOGRAPHY ON EPICTETUS, ANCIENT STOICISM, AND MODERN STOICISM

THE AVAILABLE BIBLIOGRAPHY ON ANCIENT Stoicism is large and difficult to navigate. Below is an annotated list of my favorite books, particularly those that I think may be most useful to the general reader. I have also included what I think are some of the best translations of Epictetus. To complement these readings, I have added a sampler of the most useful books about modern Stoicism. I apologize in advance for the hubris of including two entries of my own. Books are in alphabetical order by author.

Lawrence Becker, *A New Stoicism*, Princeton University Press, 2017. By far the most difficult book on this list, but also the only comprehensive attempt at outlining a coherent Stoicism for the twenty-first century. I have written an author-approved, chapter-by-chapter commentary to help with the reading (https://howtobeastoic.wordpress.com /tag/a-new-stoicism/).

Liz Gloyn, *The Ethics of the Family in Seneca*, Cambridge University Press, 2017. An innovative comparative analysis of Seneca's writings, with a focus on the concept of the family as the fundamental unit where we begin to learn how to live ethically.

Margaret Graver, *Stoicism and Emotion*, University of Chicago Press, 2009. A bit more difficult than most other entries here, which is why I wrote a chapter-by-chapter, author-approved commentary on the book (https://howtobe astoic.wordpress.com/tag/stoicism-and-emotion/). The only extensive treatment of the often misunderstood take the Stoics have on emotions.

Pierre Hadot, *The Inner Citadel: The Meditations of Marcus Aurelius*, Harvard University Press, 2001. Somewhat difficult reading, but a superb discussion of Marcus Aurelius's philosophy and of the huge influence Epictetus had over it. One of the early texts that led to the modern revival of Stoicism.

Robin Hard, *Discourses, Fragments, Handbook*, Oxford University Press, 2014. In my opinion the best modern translation of the complete works of Epictetus, with excellent explanatory notes accompanying the text.

Robin Hard, *Marcus Aurelius Meditations: with Selected Correspondence*, Oxford University Press, 2011. The most accurate and readable modern translation of this classic by the philosopher-emperor. The popular Hayes version is beautiful and inspiring, but it takes some liberties with the text, so I would avoid it if you want to make sense of Marcus Aurelius in the context of Stoic philosophy, where he surely belongs.

William Irvine, *A Guide to the Good Life: The Ancient Art of Stoic Joy*, Oxford University Press, 2008. A lively and practical introduction to Stoicism, including an excellent discussion of Stoic psychological techniques. However, beware of the author's tendency toward eclecticism (mixing different philosophies of life), and be skeptical of his transformation of Epictetus's dichotomy of control into a trichotomy.

William Irvine, *The Stoic Challenge: A Philosopher's Guide to Becoming Tougher, Calmer, and More Resilient*, W. W. Norton & Company, 2019. Focused on essentially one, fundamental, Stoic "trick," also backed up by modern psychological research: the framing effect. As counterintuitive as it seems, it is up to you how to see difficult situations and setbacks, and that decision is immensely helpful in dealing more effectively with them.

Brian Johnson, *The Role Ethics of Epictetus: Stoicism in Ordinary Life*, Lexington Books, 2016. The most comprehensive and accessible treatment of Epictetus's role ethics, the notion that in life we juggle three kinds of roles: member of the human cosmopolis, multiple roles that we choose (e.g., father, friend, colleague), and multiple roles that are assigned to us by the circumstances (e.g., son, native of a certain country, member of a certain ethnicity or gender).

Anthony Long, *Epictetus: A Stoic and Socratic Guide to Life*, Clarendon Press, 2002. Long is one of the foremost scholars (and translators) of Epictetus. Here he presents a comprehensive look at Epictetus's philosophy and how it was influenced by Socrates. Includes an interesting discussion of the relation between Stoic "theology" and ethics.

Massimo Pigliucci, *How to Be a Stoic: Using Ancient Philosophy to Live a Modern Life*, Basic Books, 2017. A very personal introduction to Stoicism, structured around a series of short imaginary conversations with Epictetus and personal anecdotes. The book covers a broad range of topics, including the use of role models, how to deal with disability and mental illness, as well as how to manage anger, anxiety, and loneliness.

Massimo Pigliucci and Gregory Lopez, *A Handbook for New Stoics: How to Thrive in a World out of Your Control—52 Week-by-Week Lessons*, The Experiment, 2019. A very practical guide to Stoicism as a lived philosophy. My friend Greg and I present fifty-two exercises, drawn from original Stoic sources and organized according to Epictetus's three disciplines, that can be sampled to see whether Stoicism is actually going to be useful in your life. (Note: in the UK market the title of the book is *How to Live Like a Stoic*.)

Donald Robertson, *Stoicism and the Art of Happiness: Practical Wisdom for Everyday Life*, Teach Yourself, 2018. Provides a clear and accessible explanation of the deep connection between Stoicism and cognitive behavioral therapy, as well as a number of practical suggestions for how to implement Stoicism in your daily life.

Donald Robertson, *How to Think Like a Roman Emperor: The Stoic Philosophy of Marcus Aurelius*, St. Martin's Press, 2019. An interesting mix of philosophical biography of Marcus Aurelius and cognitive behavioral approaches to the practice of Stoicism. You'll learn valuable lessons from the life of the philosopher-emperor.

John Sellars, *The Art of Living: The Stoics on the Nature and Function of Philosophy*, Bloomsbury Academic, 2013. A well-argued discussion of philosophy conceived as "the art of living," and of how the Stoics implemented such an idea. Sellars also suggests in this book that most sections of the *Enchiridion* are organized according to the three disciplines of Epictetus, a suggestion that I followed in the Field Guide. Be forewarned: Sellars makes frequent use of Greek words for accuracy. You'll get used to them!

John Sellars, *Stoicism*, Routledge, 2014. A concise and clear introduction to the Stoic system, including excellent treatments of Stoic ethics, physics, and logic.

William Stephens, *Marcus Aurelius: A Guide for the Perplexed*, Continuum, 2011. A splendid introduction to the philosopher-emperor, situating him in his time and clearly explaining his philosophy. An invaluable companion to any reading of the *Meditations*.

Elizabeth Asmis, Shadi Bartsch, and Martha C. Nussbaum, series eds., *The Complete Works of Lucius Annaeus Seneca*, University of Chicago Press, 2010–2017, 7 volumes. A gargantuan effort by University of Chicago Press to put out entirely new translations of all available books by Seneca. The collection includes the tragedies (two volumes), writings on anger and clemency, on hardship and happiness, on how to handle benefits, on natural philosophy, and of course the 124 letters to Lucilius.

ACKNOWLEDGMENTS

I wish to sincerely thank the many colleagues and friends who have introduced me to Stoicism and taught me the inner workings of this wonderful philosophy, particularly Larry Becker (*in memoriam*), Bill Irvine, Gregory Lopez, Don Robertson, and John Sellars. Thanks to my wonderful agent, Tisse Takagi, to my patient editor, T. J. Kelleher, and to my copy editor, Lisa Reardon, without whom this labor of love would have never seen the light. And thanks especially to my wife, Jennifer, who has been my most enthusiastic supporter during this project, not to mention such an attentive editor of the manuscript itself that the final result is significantly improved because of her labor.

NOTES

I.1. Epictetus and Me

1. I had just enrolled in "Stoic Week," an annual introduction to Stoic philosophy and practice organized by modernstoicism.com. I recount the full story in my book *How to Be a Stoic*, Basic Books, 2017.

2. *Discourses* I, 1.32.

3. Origen, *Contra Celsus*, book VII, section 53, http://www.early christianwritings.com/text/origen167.html.

4. *Discourses* II, 12.24–25.

5. There is a funny and enlightening story about what happened after Epictetus's death. To set it up, I have to first quote a bit of the *Discourses* (I, 29.21) where he explains to his students how he reacted when a thief stole his night lamp:

> This is how I came to lose my lamp: the thief was better than I am in staying awake. But he acquired the lamp at a price: he became a thief for its sake, for its sake, he lost his ability to be trusted, for a lamp he became a brute. And he imagined he came out ahead!

In light of this, it's interesting to read what Lucian of Samosata (125–180 CE) wrote in his *Remarks Addressed to an Illiterate Book-Fancier* (full text here: http://www.gutenberg.org/cache/epub/6829/pg6829-images .html):

> We have instances in our own days: I believe the man is still alive who paid 3,000 drachmae for the earthenware lamp of Epictetus the Stoic.

I suppose he thought he had only to read by the light of that lamp, and the wisdom of Epictetus would be communicated to him in his dreams, and he himself assume the likeness of that venerable sage.

I must disclose that a few years ago I bought a Roman earthenware lamp from the second century, for $750. I have no reason to think it was Epictetus's. Nor do I imagine that it has made me an iota wiser.

6. "We know how to analyze arguments, and have the skill a person needs to evaluate competent logicians. But in life what do I do? What today I say is good tomorrow I will swear is bad. And the reason is that, compared to what I know about syllogisms, my knowledge and experience of life fall far behind" (*Discourses* II, 3.4–5). That must be why, notoriously, professors of moral philosophy are no more moral than average academics; see Eric Schwitzgebel and Joshua Rust, "The Moral Behavior of Ethics Professors: Relationships Among Self-Reported Behavior, Expressed Normative Attitude, and Directly Observed Behavior," *Philosophical Psychology* 27, no. 3, 2014, 293–327.

7. In Robin Hard, trans., *Epictetus—Discourses, Fragments, Handbook*, Oxford World Classics, 2014.

I.3. Stoicism 101

1. Diogenes Laertius, *Lives and Opinions of the Eminent Philosophers* VII.2–3, Delphi Classics, 2015, https://www.delphiclassics.com/shop/diogenes-laertius/.

2. A detailed list of fifty-two Stoic practices and how to implement them in your life can be found in Massimo Pigliucci and Gregory Lopez, *A Handbook for New Stoics: How to Thrive in a World out of Your Control*, The Experiment, 2019.

I.4. Epictetean Philosophy 101

1. Diogenes Laertius, *Lives and Opinions* VII.183.

2. A detailed discussion of both the dichotomy of control and the three disciplines can be found in Pierre Hadot, *The Inner Citadel: The Meditations of Marcus Aurelius*, Harvard University Press, 2001 (particularly chapters 5–8).

3. See, for instance, Seneca, *Letters* 9.13; 36.6; 51.9; 59.18; 66.22, 34, and 50; 74.1 and 19; 76.21 and 32; 82.5; 85.40; 92.24; the whole of 98;

118.4; 119.11, Delphi Classics, 2014, https://www.delphiclassics.com/shop/seneca-the-younger/.

4. Cicero, *De Finibus Bonorum et Malorum* III.22, Delphi Classics, 2014, https://www.delphiclassics.com/shop/cicero/.

5. In William Irvine, *A Guide to the Good Life: The Ancient Art of Stoic Joy*, Oxford University Press, 2008.

6. The modern empirical evidence about what makes people happy, and what doesn't actually make much of a difference to our happiness, is summarized in Richard Layard, *Happiness: Lessons from a New Science*, Penguin, 2005. As it turns out, the Stoics were onto something when they claimed that happiness comes from within, and that externals make comparatively few contributions.

7. The notion that everything is in flux and there is no permanence of objects anywhere in the cosmos is an important part of Stoic metaphysics, and derives from the pre-Socratic philosopher Heraclitus, who famously said *panta rhei*, everything changes. He argued that, for instance, we never step into the same river twice, because the river is a dynamic entity, never the same. And so are we, of course.

8. *Discourses* III, 10.

III.1. Updating Stoicism

1. *Letters to Lucilius*, 33.11.

2. *Lives and Opinions of the Eminent Philosophers*, VII.39–40.

3. *Lives and Opinions of the Eminent Philosophers*, VII.87–88.

4. In chapter 5 of Lawrence C. Becker, *A New Stoicism*, Princeton University Press, 2017.

5. *Enchiridion* 4.

6. See Peter T. Struck, *Divination and Human Nature: A Cognitive History of Intuition in Classical Antiquity*, Princeton University Press, 2018.

7. See Brad Inwood, ed., *The Cambridge Companion to the Stoics*, Cambridge University Press, 2003. In particular, chapter 6, "Stoic Theology," by Keimpe Algra, and chapter 15, "Stoicism in the Philosophical Tradition: Spinoza, Lipsius, Butler," by Anthony A. Long.

8. *Lives and Opinions of the Eminent Philosophers*, VII.135–138.

9. In *Discourses* II, 6.9–10.

10. Some modern philosophers have resurrected a similar idea, known as panpsychism. It actually comes out of the alleged impossibility

of science to solve the problem of consciousness. These colleagues think that if consciousness is "elemental," i.e., a basic property of matter, then there would be no problem with understanding consciousness. I explain here why consciousness is an eminently scientific problem: https://aeon.co/essays/consciousness-is-neither-a-spooky-mystery-nor-an-illusory-belief, and interested readers can check out my discussion on panpsychism with Philip Goff, one of the most prominent supporters of the idea: https://letter.wiki/conversation/277.

11. The Stoics had a number of additional arguments to support their theology, but the one from design is by far the strongest. The others are described by Cicero in Book II of *De Natura Deorum* (Delphi Classics, 2014, https://www.delphiclassics.com/shop/cicero/) on the nature of the gods.

12. *Discourses* I, 6.

13. This is a good example of contemporary first philosophy–type metaphysics: David Chalmers, David Manley, and Ryan Wassermann, eds., *Metametaphysics: New Essays on the Foundations of Ontology*, Oxford University Press, 2009. And here is a good example of the alternative approach, which I favor: Don Ross, James Ladyman, and Harold Kincaid, eds., *Scientific Metaphysics*, Oxford University Press, 2015.

14. I mentioned political commitments as well, so let me expand on that briefly: I do *not* think that Stoicism implies a specific view of politics, e.g., a progressive-liberal one. Someone can be a genuine practitioner of Stoicism and yet embrace any of a number of political ideologies or positions, including libertarianism (as understood in the US, known as classical liberalism in Europe) and conservatism. However, just as in the case of metaphysics discussed in the main text, there are limits: I simply cannot coherently picture in my mind a Stoic, or virtuous, fascist.

15. For example, *Enchiridion* 12, 14, 26, and 29.

16. *Enchiridion* 30.

17. *Enchiridion* 33.

18. For the philosophically curious: When I say that humanity has made moral progress, I do not mean to endorse any metaphysically strong sense of "progress." I do not, for instance, believe that moral truths are "out there" to be discovered, and that they exist in a mind-independent manner. (That is, I'm not what philosophers call a moral realist.) I think morality is a human invention. But I also think it is constrained

by empirical facts about human nature, particularly facts regarding what human beings want and why, what makes for a flourishing life, and so on. To use an analogy, think of the evolution of (and constant progress in) airplane design: Airplanes are human inventions, they wouldn't exist apart from human beings. But their design and capabilities are constrained by the laws of physics. The more we discover, empirically, about human nature, and the more we reflect, philosophically, on the problem of living a life worth living, the more "progress" we are likely to make. This position, I think, is perfectly in line with the Stoic approach, and underlies their insistence that in order to live a eudaemonic life (ethics) we need to reason correctly (logic) and to learn about how the world works ("physics").

19. Seneca, *To Marcia, on Consolation* XVI, Delphi Classics, 2014, https://www.delphiclassics.com/shop/seneca-the-younger/.

20. Seneca, *Letters to Lucilius* XLVII, Delphi Classics, 2014, https://www.delphiclassics.com/shop/seneca-the-younger/.

21. "They declare that [the sage] alone is free and bad men are slaves, freedom being power of independent action, whereas slavery is privation of the same; though indeed there is also a second form of slavery consisting in subordination, and a third which implies possession of the slave as well as his subordination; the correlative of such servitude being lordship; and this too is evil" (Diogenes Laertius, *Lives and Opinions* VII.1.121–122).

22. Emily McGill and Scott Aikin, *Stoicism, Feminism, and Autonomy*, *Symposion* 1, no. 1, 2014, 9–24.

23. See Massimo Pigliucci, "When I Help You, I Also Help Myself: On Being a Cosmopolitan," *Aeon*, https://aeon.co/ideas/when-i-help-you-i-also-help-myself-on-being-a-cosmopolitan.

III.2. This Is Not the First Time, and It Won't Be the Last

1. See John Sellars, ed., *The Routledge Handbook of the Stoic Tradition*, Routledge, 2016.

Simon Wardenier

Massimo Pigliucci is the K. D. Irani Professor of Philosophy at the City College of New York. The author or editor of thirteen books, he has been published in the *New York Times*, *Wall Street Journal*, *Philosophy Now*, and *The Philosophers' Magazine*, among others. He lives in New York City. He blogs at massimopigliucci.com.